Matrix
of
Illusions

Dr. Angela Barnett & Joe Barnett, M.A.

Matrix of Illusions
by Dr. Angela Barnett & Joe Barnett, M.A.

ISBN-13: 978-1523881239   ISBN-10: 1523881232

For information about and purchase of the Matrix of Illusions and other books and training by the authors, go to the authors' company website
http://www.CrystalMagicOrchestra.com

Cover art and design by Joe Barnett.

Table of Contents

What is the Matrix?
The Matrix of Reality, The Matrix of Illusions, Returning to the Matrix of Reality

The Turkish Adventure
Escaping Turkish Prison, How We Barely Escaped Wrongful Persecution, Illusion or Reality?, Relationships, Divine Insights and Guidance, Divine Direction, Life Force Protection, Untouched by the Matrix of Illusions, Timing, Supply, Right Place, Epilog

The Turkish Adventure II
Are you Suicidal?, Creating Psychopaths, Creating Moral Idiots, Using Relationships, The Moral Confusion of Ethics, Give Me an A or You're Dead, Who are the Real Teachers?, Epilog

The Turkish Adventure III
Challenge of Breathing Poison, Challenge of Being Woken at Night, The Flood, Challenge of the Conspiring Principal, What was the Victory?, The Three Day Retreat, Sacrificing Everything We Owned, Loss is Gain , Did We have an Enjoyable Time in Turkey?, Epilog

From the Visible to the Invisible
Rationalizing the World, Crossing Over, Aren't We Capable of More?, Levels of Consciousness, Culture Shock, Epilog

Words, The Question of Timing, Evaluations, Other Points to Consider, Epilog

Quantum Odyssey

Creating God's Movie, The World's Movie, Aligning our Spiritual Reality , Explaining the Unexplainable, The Movie, Making God's Movie

Mindshifts

Mental mapping, Culture Shock, Family Culture, Cultural Mythology, Epilog

Culture Shock

Japanese Culture Shock, Creating Music that goes Beyond Culture, Cultural Blindspots, Epilog

Divine Mission

Who We Really Are, Aliens on Earth, Staying in the Divine Matrix of Virtual Reality , How to Survive on Earth, Programmed Reality, Making Divine Love's Movie, Love is Kind, Removing the Challenge, The Non Power

Dear Fellow Aliens

Shape Shifters, My Blueprint on Earth, Fear, Matrix of Reality, The Journey, Blueprint Themes for Success, Desire to Help

About the Authors

The authors of this book, Dr. Angela Barnett and Joe Barnett, M.A. have lived all over world as they were given spiritual guidance step-by-step to find all of the answers leading to their massive understanding of God's Movie. While spending most of their time in Asia because of unresolved issues from past lives, they also found important spiritual teachings while living in the Mediterranean and in the Caribbean Islands. Through the authors' journey as University Professors, they have taught in several universities in Japan, Korea, Puerto Rico and Turkey. They have utilized their spiritual healing to stop gang violence and murders in Universities by teaching students their true desire to have peace and harmony. Their magical ability to raise classrooms full of students grade point to an A average was highly regarded in the rest of the world, but so greatly frowned upon by American Universities and even International Schools that were governed by an American Principal, that they have found their true calling in writing books about the spiritual realities involving people's intelligence and the cultural barriers that are blocking the reality of God's children from being allowed to project and express their true being.

The Barnetts have also worked as Corporate Training Consultants and conducted research in Multinational Corporations around the world, including Amdahl,/Fujitsu, Tokiwa, Nishi Nihong Dinseng, Samsung, Hyundai and Mazda. They have written many training manuals, books and published journal articles on the Authentic Communication that is required for different cultures to work together harmoniously in the international environment. Their Masters Degrees and Doctorate are results of decades of experiential research within corporations and classrooms to uncover the mysteries of human interaction and communication and what lies much deeper behind the meanings that are shared and misunderstood when people try to communicate. They have become experts on many Asian cultures and the corporate cultures and education systems that have evolved from these cultures.

The Barnetts have come in contact with people from many spiritual persuasions including masters of Buddhism, Hinduism, Shintoism, Shamanism, as well as Muslim and many cultural varieties of Christians. They have synthesized their interest in cultural anthropology, Eastern and Western philosophy, intercultural psychology, mysticism, spiritual perceptions and lifetime of spiritual healing to transcend all cultural diversity and gain deep insights into the mysterious coincidences that occur in each of our lives. From their years of worldwide exposure to and experience with International Masters and the constant protection given by the Ascended Masters and Angels, they have found a commonality about spiritual growth along a spiritual path that transcends the specifics of any one religious belief. While communicating with the host people of each culture they lived and worked in, they concentrated on the art of Authentic Communication in order to uncover the Authentic Power in people all over the world. This Spiritual Art allowed them to escape hundreds of tragedies and to live peacefully among the host people and to give spiritual guidance to others.

The authors are also composers of healing music and authors of many spiritual books that incorporate their background of healing through spiritual understanding of the spiritual man that appears when God's movie is being projected through the eyes of the healer. They have both received their undergraduate degrees in Music and have performed professionally internationally. They performed on national T.V. stations in Korea and in Japan. The special healing music that takes on a form that is very special to the people of Japan was created for the specific reason of sharing their highest understanding of a Universal God with the people of Japan.

The authors have also designed a series of online healing workshops entitled the Quantum Journey modules and The Oneness Kit. They have authored hundreds of published articles nationally and internationally and they have been keynote speakers at many international conventions. The Matrix of Illusions contains the authors' personal spiritual journeys that have led to their highest understanding of God's movie.

Their current work, books, e-books, audio books, training, online training, and music are available through their company website - Crystal Magic Orchestra at: http://www.CrystalMagicOrchestra.com

Introduction

The Matrix of Illusions shares the miraculous accounts of healings that the Barnetts experienced, encountered and utilized during their international adventures. Incredible encounters were made that allowed Angela Barnett's vibrational level of consciousness to rise above the normal physical levels where death would be inevitable when the same poison was swallowed by those who have not yet expanded their consciousness to the sixth or seventh level where immortality reigns. The true experiences, including a close escape from being locked in a Turkish Prison, are shown to be examples of Joe Barnett's state of consciousness where he was able to remain in God's movie instead of being pulled into someone else's self-fulfilling mortal dream of existence. These and other equally awe inspiring events were the day-to-day experiences of these prophets during their international journey.

These miraculous encounters are utilized to share with the reading audience the magical and powerful freedom that belongs to those who train their minds to remain free from the Matrix of Illusions. The maintaining, reconstructing or returning to the Divine Creation of God's Movie is available to all. The experiences of the Barnett's prove that God's movie is always playing in Divine Consciousness.

Chapter 1

What is The Matrix?

The Matrix of Reality

Many people on earth think they are living in the Divine
Matrix of Reality when they are actually living in the Matrix of
Illusions. Each person needs to examine their thoughts each
day to make sure their thoughts are reflecting Divine Reality
rather than the illusions that the world would like to implant
in our minds. The master can only see perfection in everyone
and everything in the world. We are all masters. We all have
the ability to return to the Divine Matrix of Reality where we
live in the Now of Divine Perfection. We contain and we
portray the isness of eternity. There is no other reality than
the Divine Reality, and therefore we have never really left our
Divine Creation.

The Matrix of Illusions

The Matrix of Illusions can easily be mistaken for the Matrix
of Reality because to those only trained in material concepts,

these mortal dreams are the only reality available to their consciousness. Often, those who do not have a spiritually directed background cannot see the difference between spiritual reality and material reality because spiritual reality is outside of their consciousness and cannot be seen - those who have eyes, yet cannot see. The master is living, moving, and existing within and from the Divine Matrix of Reality.

The program that we have created here on earth has separated us from the original Garden of Eden, where every spiritual reality was already prepared for us. We have chosen to have control of our own world. We have become brainwashed to believe that this is the actual world that we were created in and live in, when in fact it is only a program of our minds that has been connected through electronic vibrations to lower us into the dream of material sense. When the vibrations are raised back to the speed of light, (which is what our real vibrations are) we return to our state of oneness with our true creation.

Returning to the Matrix of Reality

There are many ways of returning from the Matrix of Illusions to the Matrix of Reality. This can be done by returning to Before the World began where the Promise of the Perfect Kingdom has already been established as the reality that we can maintain, return to or reconstruct whenever our Consciousness is spiritually prepared to become all that it really is. We can help maintain the Divine Reality by staying in the Now Zone. We can reconstruct the Divine Reality by pulling out all of the roots from the Garden of Eden in which we ate of the tree of good and evil, and planting them back in the Divine Creation. The Quantum Journey writings and courses by the authors have examined in detail the ways we can return to our Divine Right of the Perfect Kingdom and how to do it.

This book, Matrix of Illusions, shows how the Matrix of Illusions works and how to recognize the different Matrices so we can be alert to them and avoid being hypnotized by them, in order to become truly free. If you don't protect yourself from the hypnotic illusions, you can and probably will be entranced and trapped by them. This book is for those who are just starting out on a spiritual path and it is also for those who have spent a lifetime on the path. Everyone can and will benefit from this book if the reader seriously looks at how s/he is being influenced by the Matrix of Illusions and works on freeing the consciousness from the erroneous influence. The matrices go much deeper and are much more pervasive than one might imagine.

As you read this book, keep an open mind before making any judgments. The many Matrices of Illusions have worked very hard at making people believe that one thing is considered good and another bad when, in actuality, the entire construct is a dream from the beginning. You might want to even hold all judgment until the entire book is finished, so you can go back and see how it all relates.

The Matrices of Illusions seem to be created by humans and at the same time often appear to have universal and Godlike qualities. However, they are only impersonal constructs that people often call "reality" and follow them because they don't know any better. Christ Jesus said, "Forgive them for they know not what they do." They do not know what they do because they think they are doing the right thing because a Matrix of Illusions brainwashed them into believing that they are right - even to the point of killing others for no reason. A Matrix of Illusions motivated the people during Jesus' time to hang Him on the cross. A Matrix of Illusions also caused the words of Jesus to be mistranslated so that we all believe the story is about something entirely opposite than what is actually about.

Many people on earth think they are living in the Divine Matrix of Reality when in fact they are living in the Matrix of Illusions. For this reason, it is necessary to be able to recognize the Matrix of Illusions and how it works to hypnotize people down into its dream. Once the Matrixes of Illusions are recognized, it becomes possible to push these beliefs, cultures and ideologies outside the doors of one's consciousness and allow Divine Creation to be lived out from. This is possible because Divine Reality is the only reality and the Matrices of Illusions are just that - illusions.

Chapter 2

The Turkish Adventure

Escaping Turkish Prison

The following true adventure is intended to help each reader examine the possibility that the themes, trials and accomplishments that have been written into their own blueprints of life on earth are the essential tools and guides necessary for helping them to achieve the victory of their plan that they wrote into their own blueprint before leaving the other side, in order to come to earth for the fulfillment of their own life journey. It is hoped that by looking at events in someone else's life and learning to see the difference between the Illusions and the Reality, that you will begin to do the same thing with each event in your own life.

How We Barely Escaped Wrongful Persecution

Waiting alone in Cyprus, and not knowing if my husband would be locked in a Turkish prison, I prayed night and day until he finally returned. Someone sent me a letter today asking for prayer and contributions for those who have been locked away in foreign prisons unlawfully. This brought back the intense memory of the time I spent a weekend on the mystical island of Cyprus, praying for the safe return of my husband, Joe, from Turkey when he was faced with a situation that we both knew could wrongfully put him in a Turkish prison.

The adventure started as a simple teaching assignment at an International School in Bebek, Turkey - a beautiful section of Istanbul. The situation turned when the Principal was thought to be embezzling money, up to about one million U.S. dollars a year, and the Principal began a cover-up through threats, the Principle's office fire that curiously only burned up the financial records filing cabinet, espionage, blocked bank accounts and attempts to turn us into illegal aliens. I will share the events surrounding our time at the school and our first apartment that almost killed us by burning unrefined coal after I explain how our second apartment got flooded, our landlord attempted to steal everything we owned and raise the rent after he flooded our apartment, our bank account was almost emptied, and how Joe finally escaped from a time in a Turkish prison with a little help from Rambo.

We had been engulfed in an ocean of unlawful acts towards us in Bebek, Turkey. The Principal of the International School placed us in an apartment near the romantic Bebek harbor and we began teaching at the school. The first thing we learned about the Principal was that all of the financial files had been mysteriously burned in her office filing cabinet just weeks earlier. "Luckily only the filing cabinet burned, so there was no damage to the building," she told us on our tour of the school. She was obviously embezzling money through her son who frequently flew in to meet her at the airport, yet only stayed for twenty minutes before catching the next flight out. The school was the most expensive International School in Turkey (and in Europe for that matter), catering to foreign diplomats and businessmen. However, there only seemed to be enough funds available to teach music with a box of broken sticks and an ill-tuned piano. When the parents complained of the piano not being tuned, the Principal accused me of stirring up trouble. Finally we found out that she had even hired us illegally and wasn't planning on getting a working visa for us.

On top of this problem, one morning we woke up almost dead in our apartment because of the burning of unrefined coal in our apartment. We stayed with a friend while we found a new apartment. Later, our new apartment, which we had completely refurnished with wall paper, rugs, drapes, all kitchen appliances, major appliances and furniture had become completely flooded due to bad plumbing which the owner was responsible for. We waded around in water six inches deep, trying to save as much furniture as possible by piling it in a corner. When we told the owner we couldn't live in that wet place, he told us that he was going to raise the rent because the place was so much improved from our refurnishing and that he would charge us rent for the remainder of the year and that he had also decided that the furniture and major appliances we purchased belonged to him.

At the same time this happened, we learned that our employer, had hired us illegally and we needed to exit the country to get our passport updated because we could be thrown in jail as illegal aliens. We prepared to fly to the nearby island of Cyprus to solve the first problem, and then Joe would fly back to Turkey to pick up our belongings later. When we went to the bank to get the money that we had been paid, the banker said we would need to wait while he made some phone calls. We felt that something was very suspicious and assumed this would be the opportune time for our employer to have us arrested as illegal aliens and refuse to pay us and then embezzle our pay for the year. The bank officer returned and stated that there was no U.S. money in the bank, so we should come back the next morning just when they open.

We left the bank immediately without our money and went straight to the airport after quickly packing an overnight bag. We later got our money out of the Turkish bank branch in downtown Istanbul that wasn't under the influence of our employer. We flew to the island of Cyprus and found an enchanting villa in which we rented an apartment. Joe then returned to Istanbul to take care of our move. I remained in Cyprus praying night and day while waiting for Joe, that he would not be locked away in a Turkish prison.

Joe's return plane ticket gave him three days to completely pack up our apartment and get moved out. He learned that professional movers would charge $4000 to move our belongings back to the U.S. - a price we could not afford. After packing twenty boxes of our books he found a Turkish friend that arranged to have the books donated to a Turkish University Library. Then he packed our clothes into two suitcases. The third day his plane was to return to Cyprus; however, he had to check into the airport by 2:00 p.m. in order to board the plane. That last morning was the time he had remaining to sell and remove our furniture from the apartment.

Totally uncertain of his future, Joe walked the streets of Istanbul's furniture and appliance district trying to find someone to purchase our new/used furniture and major appliances. He asked many shop owners all morning with no luck. After 11:00 a.m., he was directed intuitively to wander into a small electric shop where they sold toasters and other small electronic items. The owner of the shop started chatting with Joe and they continued a forty-minute chat over tea as Joe pondered how he was going to get his furniture sold and get to the plane on time - it was already nearing noon. The owner of the shop asked him to wait and then left the building for over thirty minutes. Some benevolent force kept pulling Joe back from leaving the shop. When the owner finally returned he said "I want to buy all of the furniture and appliances you own to give to a young newly married couple who has no furniture. The young man works for me, and I want to give it to him as a wedding present." They made the deal.

Before they got out the door, a big truck pulled up with a huge muscle-bound man driving it. The owner gave the money to Joe and the bill of receipt that was proof that the furniture no longer belonged to Joe. When Joe, and the young "newlywed" man jumped into the truck with the driver, he saw a picture of Rambo hanging from the truck's rearview mirror. The driver pointed to the picture and said that he liked Rambo.

The huge man that we now call Rambo, carried all of the furniture from our apartment, putting it in his truck. The young man and Joe helped. Our greedy landlord came with a crooked Turkish police officer friend claiming Joe was stealing his furniture and that Joe owed him for rent, which came to 2,000 U.S. dollars. The local real estate man that rented the apartment to us showed up on the scene after he heard the landlord yelling in the streets and stated to the landlord and the police officer that Joe did not owe the landlord rent, but the landlord and police officer continued. Joe also showed the policeman the bill of sale to prove that this was now the young Turkish man's furniture. The police officer agreed that the furniture and appliances now belonged to the young man, so after much grumbling they gave up on that. The landlord then told Rambo that he and the police officer were going to wait in the police car down on the main road and they would follow us back to the electric shop where they would settle this.

Rambo told Joe not to worry - he had a plan. He said the landlord had no right to do such a thing. They finished loading the truck and Rambo drove down the street, but instead of turning onto the main road, he quickly turned down a narrow alley that went up and over the hill a back way leaving the landlord and crooked cop waiting in the police car on the main road.

By this time, Joe was glad to be on his way back to Cyprus and free from the plot of imprisonment by both the Principal and the landlord. When Rambo dropped him off at our friend's house we had been staying at, he only had thirty minutes to get to the airport. The minute he got to the apartment one more divine coincidence happened. A friend of ours from India drove up in a stretch limo at that moment and took Joe directly to the airport. Joe arrived at the airport check-in counter a few minutes before 2:00 p.m.

I was still waiting and praying back in Cyprus late after midnight wondering if he would ever return. Finally the door opened and I couldn't believe my eyes, it was Joe.

Write in Your Journal

1. Describe the healings that you can see realized in this situation.

2. Describe the differences of the story in the Matrix of Illusions and then in the Matrix of Reality.

3. Describe the function of the Life Force in each event of the day.

Illusion or Reality?

Was this incident a part of the Matrix of Illusions or a part of the Matrix of Reality? If this incident had happened to someone who was not being directed by the Life Force, the results probably would be much different. There was a report of an U.S. person who was simply doing his job in Turkey who got framed in a similar manner, who did get locked up in a Turkish prison, and his wife spent several years trying to get him out.

Our situation in Turkey turned out better than just an escape with the threads of a shirt on our back. We were directed to not go back to that local bank the next morning and were directed to leave the country that night and go to Cyprus before going back to take care of things. This was protection. Joe was not only able to sell all of the belongings in our home; in addition, he was able to sell them to someone who really needed them for their own beginning in life, at a great discount to them. In return for the service that was being done for them, the electronic store owner helped supply the protection needed from the greedy landlord by giving a receipt written in Turkish for the household goods along with the presence of the new owner and by hiring Rambo to be there. This protection appeared as a reflection of the protection and guidance of the Life Force. Joe was guided to the electronic store through Divine Direction. Joe was guided and directly told by an Angel to wait for a very long time at the electronic store - over an hour, even though to the material sense of things, he was wasting his last couple of hours, in country, chit-chatting with the store owner about soccer and other casual topics when he needed to be out looking for someone to buy our things. The store owner gave no indication that he was interested in or was going to buy our belongings until the very last minute. The store owner also hired Rambo to pick up the young man's new things, and Rambo was also an avenue of protection for Joe. Without Rambo, things would have turned out very differently.

What other proof was there of having our consciousness in the Divine Reality instead of the Matrix of Illusions? When Joe arrived back at the friend's apartment that we were staying at, another friend drove up in her chauffeur driven limo to say good-bye. Joe didn't even need to pick up the phone to call for a taxi. If Joe's mind had been lost in the confusion of the Matrix of Illusions, he may have very well not been able to get a taxi, and he might have missed the plane.

All of these events may have been miracles to the material sense that lives in the Matrix of Illusions; however, when the mind is stayed on the Divine Qualities of spiritual sense where the Life Force is allowed to enter in and guide one as if they were riding on a Universal Surge of White Light Energy, everything falls into place as a natural fact.

Write in Your Journal

1. Describe the healings that you can see happening during this day in Turkey?

2. What healings do you see resulting from the relationship between the furniture store owner, the young married couple, Rambo, the police and the landlord?

3. What healings do you see resulting from the intercultural insights about this culture?

4. What healings do you see resulting from intuition and guidance?

5. What healings do you see resulting from Divine Direction?

6. What healings do you see resulting from allowing the Life Force to lift us into the Universal Energy where the poison of carbon monoxide could not penetrate our body?

7. What healings do you see resulting from the Divine Timing?

8. What healings do you see resulting from those remaining in the Matrix of Illusions being unable to touch our lives?

9. What healings do you see of Abundance of Supply?

10. What healings do you see of Right Place?

Relationships

When we are guided by the Life Force, all Divine Relationships appear as they are needed. It was the Divine Love Life Force providing the already perfect plan of Oneness. When we see ourselves as One with the Universe, and expand our desires or needs to include the needs of all, the answers to our prayers are answered by making someone else's dreams come true as well as our own. The real miracle here was not that we were able to get our belongings out of the house we were renting from a landlord who refused to take responsibility for flooding our home and wanting to steal our belongings and extort money from us. The real miracle was that there was someone who needed the furniture, the refrigerator, washer, drapes, etc. that we had just purchased a few months earlier. How nice it was that this newly wed couple who had no money of their own would be able to completely furnish their apartment with some very nice things. This is how Divine Love works. Divine Love works in a universal manner including everyone involved.

The reason the big man with the truck was so helpful was also twofold. This man was also friends with the electronic store owner who wanted to help the young married couple. The man we called Rambo was also very strong and able to move the furniture in a very short time. The man also was very wise to the landlord's tricks because these tricks are universal. The tricks were lined with greed and corruption and taking advantage of people. Rambo had seen all of these tricks before in the furniture moving business. Rambo knew the rights of ownership and jurisdiction. He knew that since we had already signed a bill of sale, that the ownership of the furniture was no longer in our name, that furniture belonged to his friends. This was the divine relationship that was protecting us from the landlord's lies and demands.

Write in Your Journal

1. Write down your own experiences with Divine Relationships.

Divine Insights and Guidance

The event of Divine Guidance during this day included the document that been signed proving that the furniture belonged to a Turkish citizen, was proof that the landlord could not say the furniture belonged to him. Rambo was also like a spirit guide showing us that all we needed to do to avoid the landlord's harassment and to keep from getting thrown in a Turkish prison was to drive the already loaded truck out the back road instead of down to the main road where the landlord and policeman were waiting to arrest Joe in order to extort money from us.

Write in Your Journal

1. Write down your own experiences with Divine Insights and Guidance.

Divine Direction

Where did the direction come from that led Joe into the electronic store where all of this divine protection would come from? It was Divine Direction that flows through anyone who is listening for guidance. How did Joe know that this was Divine Direction? How did he know he should sit there, drink tea and wait for the store owner instead of continuing to search through the city for someone to sell our belongings to? It came as a quiet thought and nudge to go into the store at first even though a small appliance store would not be interested in buying our furniture and major appliances. Then as they were talking, Joe felt that maybe he should leave and a quiet inner voice told him directly to wait and be patient and enjoy talking with this fellow. After the fellow asked Joe to wait and left the building, Joe once again thought that maybe he should be moving on after the fellow did not return after twenty minutes. When Joe was about to stand up, once again, the inner voice told him directly, quietly and with strength and power to sit and wait for the shop owner. There is always a feeling of Divine Protection and completeness accompanying Divine Direction. It never comes from reason or logic or time. It often comes in direct denial of logic and time. In the Matrix of Illusions the most logical thing to do would be to not wait around, chit-chat and drink tea with a man when there were only a few hours left before leaving on the plane out of the country. Divine Direction always comes at the last second, when it is needed because it doesn't know time the way it is thought of in the material sense. Direction comes when it is supposed to come, not when we think it should come.

Write in Your Journal

1. Write down your own experiences with Divine Direction.

Life Force Protection

The protection of the life force was already evident through the direction to the electronic store, answering the needs of the young married couple, and finally having Rambo drive the truck out the back, down a dirt road while the police were waiting on the other side of the hill, down on the main road. A part of the protection was extended through the landlord and policeman themselves by being in the wrong place at the wrong time. The police and the landlord were in the Matrix of Illusions while those making the Divine Plan of Action happen were in the Matrix of Reality. In this reality, the bad guys cannot enter the movie of Divine Reality because they are in a different movie.

Write in Your Journal

1. Write down your own experiences with Divine Protection.

Untouched by the Matrix of Illusions

The reason that Joe was untouched by the Matrix of Illusions
was because he was in the movie of the Matrix of Reality.
These two movies cannot play in the same consciousness at
the same time. As long as we are playing God's movie, the
movies of those who are still in the Matrix of Illusions cannot
interfere with the movie we prepared in our blueprints on the
other side. Those in the Matrix of Illusions know nothing of
the Divine Plan and they cannot raise their level of vibrations
to the place of insight and awareness needed to understand
or even become a part of those at a different level of
consciousness. There are no bad guys in the good guy movie.

Write in Your Journal

1. Write down your own experiences of being untouched by
the Matrix of Illusions.

Timing

There is no time in Divine Activity. There is only the speed of
light. Joe didn't need to place an add in the Turkish
newspaper a month ahead of time to sell the furniture in the
apartment. He didn't even need to go to more than one store
to complete the activity. Rambo didn't need extra manpower
or extra time to remove all of the furniture from the
apartment; he did his job at the speed of light like an action
movie animation. The only people not moving at the speed of
light were the landlord and the policemen because they were
not in the speed of light movie.

The timing continued to be perfect as Joe arrived back at the
friend's apartment we were temporarily staying at. Another
friend drove up in her chauffeur driven limo only seconds
after Joe had arrived to get the suitcases. Joe didn't even need
to pick up a phone to call a taxi. The limo driver chose the
proper route to get to the airport in a very short time, and the

airplane took off from Turkey and arrived in Cyprus without difficulty.

Write in Your Journal

1. Write down your own experiences with Divine Time.

Supply

The supply that was needed was met for everyone involved. The young married couple got their needed furniture, and we got enough money for the furniture to help get us to our next point in life. We were able to find a wonderful condo in Cyprus to stay at for a few months while deciding what to do next. The time in Cyprus was one of the most wonderful and inspiring times of our lives. The people in Cyprus were fascinating, kind, generous and a little mysterious. It was no wonderful that some of our greatest writers go there to write their novels. It cost so little to live in Cyprus that we could have lived there for years on the little bit of money that we had. Even though we had no job and no prospect of a job we felt infinitely supplied with whatever would be our next direction in life.

Write in Your Journal

1. Write down your own experiences with Divine Supply.

Right Place

We were in the right place when we lived in Turkey. We were in the right place when we chose to leave Turkey. Joe was in the right place when he entered the electronic store, and in the right place when the police were waiting to arrest him. We were in the right place when we were in Cyprus. I was in the right place as I was waiting for Joe in Cyprus. We were in the right place when we found the perfect place to stay in Cyprus because it allowed the owners to make a little extra money while they lived on their yacht. When we didn't need to be there any more that was the right place as well. We are always in the right place when we live in and from the Divine Matrix of Reality.

Write in Your Journal

1. Describe a similar situation that has happened in your life time.

2. How many blessings in disguise can you see happening in this event?

3. How has the Life Force guided, directed, provided abundant supply, protection and healing in this event?

4. Write down your own experiences with Divine Insights, Angels and Direction.

Epilog

The Divine Insights gained from this experience are infinite. We learned about Divine Jurisdiction by placing our lives in the Divine Matrix where only justice of the Divine Force can exist. The only thing that would make the Matrix of Illusions take over would be fear, lack of intuition, blocking our minds from the guiding Angel messages, and not believing that we were always living in the Divine Protection, Divine Guidance and Divine Jurisdiction of Love.

Chapter 3

The Turkish Adventure II

Are you Suicidal?

These were the threatening words used by the "wicked witch of the west Principal" of the International School in Turkey, as she attempted to terrify my husband into believing that his career and life would be destroyed by her all powerful ability to write bad recommendations and fire him. And what had he done that was so tremendous that she would need to use such words?

She claimed that he was caught not sticking strictly to the textbook that the Principal and her committees claim to have chosen for his reading class. In reality, it is always the textbook companies who tell the schools what textbook they will use through means of pay offs, bribes, freebees, and they use threats, when they are government sponsored. So this terrible textbook that was totally unsuitable for the class being taught was the issue so important that this principal should use words like "suicidal" and, "I will fire you."

This textbook issue is so important that there is absolutely no consideration given to the fact that the students were bored, frustrated and unable to learn anything from the textbooks that the administration had chosen. Or, is this the real reason this textbook was chosen? According to the life long research of John Taylor Gatto, the textbooks are chosen to dumb down the students through boredom and tedious tasks, which will only allow them to learn absolutely nothing and burn up most of their youth to accomplish.

In fact, there has been considerable research done to show that the function of the reading textbook cause massive damage to language development. In The Underground History of American Education, Gatto shares Jerry Farber's metaphor "Student as Nigger" to show us how "if we forced children to learn to walk with the same methods we use to force them to read, a few would learn to walk well in spite of us, most would walk indifferently, without pleasure, and a portion of the remainder would not become ambulatory at all" (p. 308).

So, we can see that Joe was not the only teacher who was intelligent enough to perceive of how damaging the reading textbook was to these children. But, how many teachers have been willing to fight to remove the textbooks? And how many teachers actually believe these textbooks are teaching the children how to read? My personal question is how could anyone have a mind so twisted that they could even comprehend the nothingness of what was claimed to be taught by these textbooks. The answer to that question can be found in Gatto's extensive research on the history of U.S. education. Since the educators that stay in the system are brainwashed by the system, and are incapable of thinking beyond the possibility that whatever is put in front of them is what they should do, they certainly don't question the validity of a textbook. These teachers actually believe that education should be a type of punishment. The purpose of the school system is to make sure that these students learn as little as possible in the greatest amount of time possible.

Write in Your Journal

1. Describe the reality that comes from pointing out the truth.

2. Explain your present belief of the value of the education system.

3. Explain why you think learning should be enjoyable.

Creating Psychopaths

Gatto's chapter on the Psychopathology of Everyday Schooling shows us how the system has been created to make sure the children become pathological. Pathology is a natural by-product of our modern school system. As a result, children lack compassion, laugh at weakness, show contempt for people who need help, can't stand intimacy or frankness, masquerade behind personalities found on television, avoid close scrutiny, and grow up to be whining, treacherous, terrified, dependent adults, passive and timid in the face of new challenges; and all of this will be hidden under the mask of bravado, anger and aggressiveness. (Gatto, 2001)

Well, now we all know why psychopaths such as the Principal of this International School are so commonly found in all American schools. This is the type of person required to uphold the conspiracy of education. This is the type of person required to make sure the children and the teachers are miserable. This is the type of person required to make everyone believe that they would be committing suicide if they went against her psychopathic empire. This is the type of person who makes sure that textbooks that are proven to destroy the minds of children will be used in every classroom, and any teacher who is caught allowing a child's mind to become free from the control of such a textbook will have their career destroyed.

So, why was Mr. Gatto able to use these textbooks for so many years? And how was he able to receive best teacher of the year and outstanding teacher awards so many times?

Gatto admits that he was totally miserable for most of his public school teaching career; every morning was a painful challenge to make the decision to go to work, for he knew he would have to use the dumbing down tools administered to him if he wanted to survive. Fortunately, for people like my husband and I, there are people willing to sacrifice thirty years of their lives providing substantial proof of the things that we have clearly seen and experienced, but do not have such a vast lifetime of experience with within the U.S. public school system. And we all know that someone who has already been crowned the best teacher in the system will be listened to with respect. When a person such as myself makes a claim such as the textbooks being a total waste of time, the idiots in charge of the department and the administrators who don't care if the students are learning anything or not - who don't care if the students are not motivated, and who do not care about anything but maintaining the government's directive to keep the U.S. population stupid, will try to destroy our credibility and reputations as teachers.

Write in Your Journal

1. Describe realities that have occurred in your lifetime that would substantiate the claim that children's minds are destroyed by the education system.

2. Explain your present belief about why it would be preferable to utilize education methods that both motivate children to learn and teach them how to learn.

3. Explain your present belief about why it would be better if we did not have an education system that created psychopaths.

Creating Moral Idiots

Nobody cares if we can prove that the methods we use to teach motivate the students to learn more, make them better readers, better thinkers and more prepared for their future. According to the U.S. school system, a person who doesn't use the textbooks has no morals or ethics.

So what are morals and ethics in the U.S.? Doing the right thing? Is using a textbook that makes students unmotivated the moral and ethical thing to do? Yes, according to our self-righteous education and government system. Is there any relationship between the ethical standards a teacher is forced to uphold and the morals that Christ taught? Do unto others as you would have them do unto you?

Every U.S. person who has attended school has wished the trivia and treatment that had been placed on them had not been done unto them. And yet, as soon as they graduate, they begin doing unto their students the exact things they wished their teachers had not done unto them. Ditto for parents and all employers.

Is it possible to remain in the Matrix of Reality while teaching the Matrix of Illusions? Not in our experience. We have been motivating students and teaching students in spite of the system. How is that possible? It is possible mostly because we only teach in other countries that don't have the immoral ethical standards that maintain the U.S. education status quo. When we do teach in the U.S., we just teach the way God directs us to teach until some busy body teacher or chairman of the department finds out that our students are not getting stupid enough.

The people that do evaluations of other teachers are so stupid that if you don't look like the mirror image of them, they can't understand what you are doing. Whenever a teacher doesn't understand something, they start pointing fingers and saying everyone else is wrong, except them. And this cycle goes on and on and on. The only teachers that are capable of working in this system have absolutely no clue of how to teach or what they think, so becoming a mirror image of the moral idiot in charge makes these people content. And that is what our schools are made of, created by and maintained by - moral idiots.

Write in Your Journal

1. Explain how it is that you didn't know these things about our education system before reading this.

2. How do we all stay oblivious to what is going on right in front of our eyes?

3. How is it possible for so many parents to be unable to see what the schools are doing to their children?

Using Relationships

There may be 1% that fight for something better and don't get fired. The reason this is possible is usually because of some type of relationship or power the person has in the community or with someone on the board of directors. This was exactly how John Taylor Gatto was able to maintain his credibility without selling out totally. When you have a spouse, relative or friend who is on the Board of Directors, or President of the PTA, you may be able be a teacher and maintain some of your morals.

This is exactly what my husband did in Turkey. After the Principal had already threatened me to never speak with the PTA, my husband wrote them a long letter explaining the situation of the textbooks, the lack of motivation among the students, the refusal to tune the piano, and all of the other totally unethical standards the Principal had maintained at this school. When we made our exit from the school, leaving the PTA with all of the evidence they needed against the Principal, every parent at the school pulled their children out of the school and put them in a different school before the year was over and the school was left completely empty. It turned out that it was the Principal who was suicidal, not my husband.

Write in Your Journal

1. Describe the victory that you see resulting from telling the parents the truth about the school system.

The Moral Confusion of Ethics

As Dan Seligman stated in his Forbes article of 10/28/02 entitled Oxymoron 101, "George W. Bush . . . said in his July 9 speech on Wall Street: 'Our schools of business must be principled teachers of right and wrong, and not surrender to moral confusion and relativism.'" Students do not and cannot learn ethics from the ridiculous course objectives that have been established for teaching ethics set by the government (which all accredited schools must adhere). However, they do learn ethics from the school by the examples shown them by the school administration. President Bush seems to be unaware of the fact that teachers are not allowed to make choices in their teaching and therefore cannot be principled and remain employed at the same time.

Students do learn ethics in the classroom but not from the textbook. First they learn to be totally confused about what an ethic is from the textbooks. They are given long definitions and names of ethics that have been used throughout history. By the time they get done memorizing the history of ethics, they have no idea if one is right or wrong. Then they are mentally prepared for the corruption that is easily manipulated into minds beaten down by the U.S. education system. They learn corruption through their daily interactions with professors, administrators, counselors and all of the lack of integrity that precedes them.

Professors actually have no rights to explain or teach anything to a student outside of what the textbook says and what the course objectives dictate. If a professor tried to teach a student right from wrong, applying examples from reality, or adding an educated opinion, the administrator could then employ their daily flexible "on-the-spot-policy-making" procedure to fire the teacher. Of course, if you ask the school the question about whether they allow the teacher freedom of speech and discussions of ethics, they will make up another policy on-the-spot that gives the "right" impression. You can never get the truth out of these lying weasels.

A colleague of mine was fired recently for this exact act. He added some real life examples to explain an ethics point in a Logic and Philosophy class. The discussion of ethics cannot easily be disconnected from our government and politics because that's a big part of our cultural ethics. However, when there was only a mention of unethical politics made in this class, one student, who was extremely conservative, became very angry and reported the teacher to the Dean simply because he disagreed with what the professor had said. This teacher was not only fired, but the school had a local policeman at the door of his class to bar him from entering his class.

On top of this, when I used this example to explain to a class how impossible it was to use examples to explain something to them, a student in my class accused me of being a liar about this same issue. The student got a petition against me from the rest of the class because he was the bully running the class and insisted that he was right and I was wrong. He made me into a liar simply by bullying class members into signing a petition. And why can this be done? This student is what the education breeds and desires to breed - little Nazi terrorists. The administrators will side with these terrorists every time.

Do I have proof of this? Plenty. Gatto provides the entire history of our Prussian education system in his chapter titled The Prussian Connection. Our education system is a replication of the Prussian system created to mold soldiers who are ready to attack the enemy. Who is the enemy? Anyone who tries to change the system from the Nazi clone manufacturing farm into a humanistic learning system.

The problem with teaching ethics is it is like teaching religion. Almost everyone disagrees with everyone else about everything. Education does not give the professor the respect for knowing his/her subject as it was only two decades ago. Universities now view the paying student as the expert and his/her opinion prevails in every discussion. A professor who disagrees with the opinion of a student may be fired for behaving poorly (if a "policy-of-the-day" is quickly created by the Dean that says that).

Write in Your Journal

1. Explain your understanding of morals and ethics.

2. Do you see examples of these morals and ethics in business and society?

Give Me an A or You're Dead

A student in my class stood up from his seat on the first day of class and said that he expected to be given an "A" in this class because all of his other teachers gave him A's. When I said, "I don't just give out all A's; students have to work for their grades," this student became irate and complained to the administrators to make sure he would get his A even before the class had begun. I then received a call from the Dean telling me I had broken a school policy by telling the student that he might not get an A. This policy was made up at that very moment by that Dean. This is how all university policies are made - as they are needed. Only one week earlier this same Dean had quoted his policy to me saying that we should never guarantee A's to students. So the highest ethical standard at this university is to say whatever is needed to give the impression you want. This same Dean, in a moment of honesty, told me that he used to tell the truth but has learned to lie in order to work for the university. This means when the accreditation committee comes they are shown one set of records, when the professors come they are shown another set of records, and when the students come they are shown another set of records. This is where the business majors learn to utilize this same type of bookkeeping system when they prepare their financial records for the IRS in their companies, which allows for major embezzlement. Ethics has not been left out of education at all; poor ethics are bred into every student every day.

Teaching ethics in business that apply to the workplace will get a professor fired faster than anything. We've had to create non-profit groups such as FIRE (Freedom of Intellectual Rights in Education) in order to begin controlling the enormous problem of lack of freedom of speech in the classroom. Professors are not allowed to be principled or to teach the difference of the truth and a lie in the classroom. However, the university ethics modules do include the fact that it is considered good to lie in the workplace and that whistle blowing is considered bad; as agreed by lawyers who have defined those with the ethics to tell the truth to the government as squealers.

Write in Your Journal

1. Describe how the Matrix of Illusions is maintained through obfuscating ethics in the classroom.

Who are the Real Teachers?

There are those who truly want to teach, and there are those who merely want a career in the establishment. Those career motivated teachers do not care about raising a student's chances for survival, they only care about raising their own chances for survival, and for career advancement through whatever criteria the establishment sets. These career seekers will gladly create B and C students out of A students in order to keep their jobs. These types will gladly conspire to brainwash students with trivia from textbooks that have nothing to do with anything they will need to know in their lives. While the "real" teachers will try their best to try to relate these textbooks to something real in their lives and then be reprimanded for not "sticking to the textbook."

Gatto gives the secret of how the few survive the system while teaching something that will actually benefit the students. If you are lucky enough to have your wife running the school board, as he was, you can actually transform the system and keep your job while winning awards for being the best teacher. It is always these inside and back door connections and relationships that give and keep the jobs of teachers at every level in our society.

Most teachers who do get full time teaching positions and most part time positions go through the back door of the good old boy system of being hired because they are the son of a friend of a friend who went to high school with the superintendent of schools, or the wife of the city councilman, or the brother of the wife of the mayor's second cousin. It does not mean that they went to all of the right schools, got all of the right degrees and credentials and have had ample teaching experience with years of proven expertise, publications, outstanding awards, or any of these things. Anyone that applies solely through the front door by simply applying for the job through the administration office has almost no chance of getting a job.

Write in Your Journal

1. Write down all of the ways that you can presently conceive of that the education system is maintaining the Matrix of Illusions.

Epilog

It is the hope of the authors that each of you will accomplish a journal that restores the blue print of your intended life, and restores your identity and your purpose that you are successfully achieving by identifying the themes of your life and how you are successfully accomplishing them. You will eventually realize that the themes in your life that you set out to accomplish are just as important as the themes that Christ or Buddha set out to accomplish when they wrote their blueprints from the other side. And as other great masters have left their perfect heavenly home to leave their blueprints for us, each of us are here to do the same thing for each other.

Reference

Gatto, John Taylor (2001). The Underground History of American Education. NY: The Oxford Village Press.

Chapter 4

The Turkish Adventure III

Challenge of Breathing Poison

Every day of our lives had been met with great challenges, including breathing unrefined coal, which is something like breathing carbon-monoxide poison all night long every night we lived there. While Turks are accustomed to this unrefined coal, those foreign to this concept have had the belief of this impure coal having a toxic effect. If the Turks believed as most modern nations do, they would all be in the hospital.

We had this same challenge when we lived in Korea next to a toxic waste dump that was burning plastic. While toxic fumes almost killed us, the Koreans living in the same apartment complex were not even aware they were breathing poison.

Both of these cases are proof of the Matrix of Illusions being caused by the way we are educated to believe something has a poisonous power over us or not. In Korea and in Turkey the people have not been educated to believe that one type of air is better than another, as we have been educated in America. That doesn't mean that one education system is better than another; it just shows that we are manipulated into believing whatever the Matrix we are living in wants us to believe.

Write in Your Journal

1. Describe a situation that the education you had received caused a negative result.

2. Consider the possibility that the only reason that something makes you ill is because you have been made to believe that it does so. Can you see how that could be true? Explain why or why not you are ready to believe this is possible.

Challenge of Being Woken at Night

In this quiet little Muslim town, we were woken every morning at 2 a.m. with Muslim chanting over the loud speaker. While this was quite annoying at first, it was actually a good thing to be reminded that there was an active thought of the Divine Being's Presence being prepared.

After living with this Divine reminder in the middle of the night for the time in Turkey, I still wake up in the middle of the night two or three times to remind myself of the Divine Presence, and to know the Masters are awake with me.

Write in Your Journal

1. Describe how you would feel if you were woken every night at 2 a.m. by an annoying sound.

2. Describe how you would feel if you were woken every night a 2 a.m. to be reminded of the Divine Being's Presence.

The Flood

We moved into a new apartment located right next to the school because we almost died from the carbon-monoxide gas in the first apartment. We found a basement apartment that the landlord had done nothing with. We had to totally refurbish the old basement apartment. We had to do everything from wallpaper, carpet, drapes, refrigerator, furniture, etc. The only thing that was there was a bathtub. Only two months after we finished completely refurnishing with wallpaper, rugs, drapes, all kitchen appliances and furniture, the entire apartment flooded, due to bad plumbing, which the owner was responsible for. Water started seeping through our walls, into our electric sockets, soaking our wallpaper, then soaking our carpet, soaking all of our boxes of books and clothing. We waded around in water six inches deep, trying to save as much furniture as possible by piling it in a corner.

When we told the owner we couldn't live in that wet place, he told us that he was going to raise the rent because the place was so much improved from our refurnishing, and that he would also charge us rent for the remainder of the year and that he had decided that the furniture and appliances we purchased now belonged to him.

The loss was very great to us, but the good result was being able to help out a newly wed couple to get all of the new furniture for their home. It was divine protection that made sure the landlord didn't get to steal our furniture while having Joe erroneously arrested. The goodness that one does for others is returned greatly to those who do good. We knew there was something much more important happening to us in this situation than just losing our job and losing every thing we had invested in for our home in Turkey.

Write in Your Journal

1. Describe a similar incident that has happened in your life. Think of all of the good things that came from that incident.

Challenge of the Conspiring Principal

The U.S. Principal of the International School that we worked at caused the most painful problems for us, as she was actively conspiring and manipulating all of the teachers and parents to maintain her power and control. She even set a fire in her office to eliminate files that could be used to prove she was mismanaging and embezzling money from the school.

One day she called me into her office to interrogate and threaten me with her evil, witch-like tone, accusing me of promoting the parents to demand to have the school's piano tuned. This is the level of triteness that must be dealt with by teachers everywhere in the world. I was the music teacher, so it was obvious that the parents would talk with me about their concern that the piano was out of tune. Such a small event could be used to try to destroy a teacher who would had prepared musical programs for their children to become stars in. If a teacher gains such popularity and power in a school run by a principal who must control all elements of the environment, including passports, bank accounts, apartment rentals and textbook payoffs, the teacher must be eliminated.

Here was a prestigious, international school where the tuition of any one of the parents would have paid for the entire music program, and yet, there wasn't enough money available to tune the piano. There also wasn't enough money to have anything but a box of broken sticks to teach music classes with. The textbooks were given to the school through promotions of the textbook company to maintain the U.S. government's control of what was being taught there. The principal regularly met her son at the airport with a briefcase full of money where her son just got off the plane, took the briefcase and got on the next flight out. So, where was the good to come from?

Teachers and parents had been putting up with this type of abuse for several years before we arrived, and nobody had the courage to do anything about it. Teachers always believe that their careers will be ruined if they cross a Principal. We didn't feel that way. We knew that in the Divine Matrix that we would always find our right place and our supply. After refusing to accept the abuse and accusations made, we were also told that we would not be getting legal work visas for this teaching position. The Principal didn't want to go to the trouble of taking care of the teachers properly. Instead, she demanded that they leave the country every three months to get a new tourist visa and work illegally. On top of that, she wasn't going to allow us to leave work long enough to get our visa updated. So, a catch 22 would make us illegal aliens and get us thrown in prison. When we got this news, we immediately went to the bank to get our money out and plan a trip out of the country and back to get our visas updated in time. At the bank, the bank person made a telephone call to the Principal before answering us. The bank person then told us there were no dollars available in their bank to close out our account and that we should come back the next morning. We knew that something suspicious was up at that point, and we assumed that when we came back there the next morning there would be police waiting rather than our money. So, we packed our bags and got on the next flight out to Cyprus, so that we could return on legal tourist visas to Turkey. When Joe came back with his passport stamped, he went downtown where there was a large branch of this same bank and got our money out there. The branch manager in the downtown branch said it was ridiculous and untrue that the bank didn't have enough dollars to close out our account.

Write in Your Journal

1. Describe a situation where you were directed and divinely protected when the potential for something tragic to happen occurred.

What was the Victory?

It may appear that we had lost the battle, but won the war. Actually, the important thing that was accomplished by supporting the parent's desire to have a better music program by allowing them to know that they were being ripped off by a Principal who wouldn't even tune the piano. People were aware that there was more money being given to the school than was being used for the teaching process. We raised the level of awareness out of the Matrix of Illusions where the abuse had been taking place for years. Only six months after we left, every parent pulled their kids out of this school and put them in another school. This was a true victory for all involved.

Write in Your Journal

1. Describe the greatest victory in this situation.

The Three Day Retreat

When we arrived in Cyprus, we found an apartment, and I stayed there while Joe returned to Turkey to sell our furniture. This was when the landlord tried to accuse him of stealing our furniture from our apartment and have him arrested as a thief. I waited at our wonderful apartment in Cyprus for Joe.

I made a fire each morning in the fireplace to create some warmth downstairs and then spent most of the time wrapped in quilts to stay warm while I read the Science and Health by Mary Baker Eddy from cover to cover over and over again. This was how I kept my mind so full of Divine Omnipresence that the fear of something happening to Joe couldn't get in and I could go beyond fear to the Divine Protective work that we both needed to get through this period in time. I prayed constantly as I read to know that Joe was being directed and protected by God every step of the way, every minute of the day, and everything he needed would be supplied to him. I studied the divine meanings of Direction, Guidance, Supply, Right Place, Jurisdiction and Protection.

I did need to take a walk once a day down the hill to get some food - usually a loaf of bread and some oranges. The rest of the three days were like Christ's retreat to the mountain top, with three days of continuous prayer to prepare for the coming times.

Write in Your Journal

1. Describe how your prayer has helped guide and protect someone while they were away from you.

Sacrificing Everything We Owned

When we took the job in Turkey, we assumed that everything would be legit and legal. We assumed we were working at a real International School that is accredited by the U.S. School System. We assumed we would keep working there for several years. So, with this assumption, we had dozens of boxes full of our books, clothes, cook wear, etc. shipped by boat. When the boat arrived, we got notice and the school's Turkish janitor went with us to pick up our boxes. We went into the custom's office and waited in line at one desk at a time, and had to pay off the man at each desk $20 each to stamp a paper, which the man would stick in his pocket as a bribe to get the job done. Finally, after getting all of the papers stamped so we could get the boxes off of the boat, the man on the docks wasn't going to give us our boxes unless we paid him off and let him have some of our books.

Write in Your Journal

1. Describe how the actions taken at this customs office could possibly be considered legal and appropriate.

2. What do we need to do to be able to raise our thoughts beyond judgment of right and wrong and allow the is-ness of the situation to be the only thing we see.

Loss is Gain

Less than a year later, when it was time to leave Turkey, we learned that there was no way to get our books and things we owned out of the country for less than $4000. Since everything we owned wasn't worth nearly that much, we decided to sell as much as we could. We had an entire library full of books, and the Turkish University had a library with very few books. A Turkish friend arranged to have all of our books donated to the Turkish library.

Our loss was someone else's gain. Remember, in the Matrix of Reality, there is only One, so one's gain is everyone's gain.

Write in Your Journal

1. If we are all One, is it possible to have a real victory unless many share the victory?

2. Describe how your prayers are answered when they are for a selfish purpose.

3. Describe how your prayers are answered when they are for the good of many.

Did We have an Enjoyable Time in Turkey?

We had a spectacular time in Turkey. Please remember that none of the events that are being described here are in our movie in the Matrix of Reality. There were people continuously trying to paint a movie in the Matrix of Illusions, but this wasn't the focus of our experience. I might add that there was only a few people causing bad things to happen. Everyone else in Turkey was absolutely wonderful.

The things we remember most about living in the little town of Bebek, located in the Istanbul metropolitan area, were the daily walks we took along the Bosphorous River, stopping to have their delicious baklava or ice cream or chocolate candy - the best in the world. The atmosphere was extremely romantic, the people were charming, the theme was international. There was never a feeling of being at a loss of anything because there was so much of everything for so little. I could go to the butcher and order steaks by the pound that cost less than we are used to paying for a hamburger in the U.S. It was always fun shopping at the produce stores and collecting beets, onions, potatoes and cabbage to add to the steak in making the most delicious borsch the mouth could imagine. We enjoyed spending our weekends taking boat cruises to surrounding areas, riding in horse driven carts, walking along the docks exploring the old pirate ships, sipping tea in 700 year old inns and exploring the ancient places where Christ's mother had lived.

I will never forget the day the rain was pouring down and I didn't have my key. I knocked on the door of a neighbor and they invited me in as if I were their own family, prepared me dinner, tea, dry clothes, and a bed to sleep in until my husband came home. I have never experienced hospitality like this in my home country. It has been a custom historically for travelers in Muslim countries to be able to knock on doors when shelter is needed. This is why Jesus could roam the country as he did without worrying about where he would lay his head each night or receive his next meal.

There were so many wonderful things about this country, that it seemed that the one landlord was not a typical Turk. The Principal was from the U.S., and was actually rather typical as far as my experiences have been with U.S. school administrators.

Write in Your Journal

1. Describe the healings that you can see realized in this situation.

2. Describe the differences of the story in the Matrix of Illusions and then in the Matrix of Reality.

3. Describe the function of the Life Force in each event of the day.

4. Describe the life themes that you have set out to accomplish.

Epilog

The only reason that life on earth would appear to be, or turn out to be less than fruitful, or even painful is because we have been trained to look at life through someone else's blueprints instead of the ones that we personally designed for ourselves, for whatever purpose it was that we wanted to fulfill. If we have designed blueprints for some architectural design where we expect to live in a mansion with many rooms, but the builder decides to build our home from a blueprint of a dark cave, we are not going to be very happy in our new home. This is exactly what each of us does to ourselves. We have already designed the plan that we want to live through before we leave the other side, and yet when we get here we sometimes become hypnotized and manipulated by the world to follow someone else's blueprints.

Chapter 5

From the Visible to the Invisible

No spaceships, no anecdotes, just a true story of how we are all aliens conforming to a culture that isn't really ours. Until a person has experienced the vivid mind altering process associated with culture shock to the tenth degree, they are virtually hypnotized into a world that doesn't even exist.

"Wake up Neo . . . the Matrix has you." - The Matrix

We are trapped into a Mindset that never changes or expands beyond the tiny little reality that our society, education and religions box us into. Every time I begin a new class in which I share my international travels and horrific experiences, the audience glares with mouths wide open, creating the expression, "I can't believe this is true," on their face. Why do we have such a hard time believing something we haven't experienced? My experience on this earth has led me to believe we are a culture lacking empathy. Most people don't even know what empathy means, and never attempt to learn what it means.

There are those who speak to me and I listen, and yet I do not understand why they say what they say. Then I listen to the silence between the words. I hear the voice of Love speaking inside of me and inside of him/her. There is authentic communication that helps me know Divine Mind's voice is in man, even when I don't understand a word s/he is saying.

Traveling between the physical world of quantum physics to the spiritual world of virtual reality allows us to see and hear the voices in the silent spaces, the visions that our physical senses only give a hint of. The beauty of the rose is only a speck of the eternal beauty on the Virtual side. The more we are willing to give up the illusions of the physical, the more we will enjoy the Virtual Reality of a spiritual creation.

To become empathetic to someone else's experience, we must try to see the experience from the other person's perspective. That means when the person is trying to explain to you how cold it is in Korea in the winter time, you don't hold the image in your mind of how cold it is in California. Since California is the only place you have experienced a winter, your mind is trapping you from be coming empathetic to the person telling you about the winter in Korea. The only thing your mind tells you is, " I don't know, I've never experienced 20 below zero coldness, but I remember this time I got cold when I went skiing at Lake Tahoe." I remember every time I called home from Japan, if I told someone that it was very humid in Japan, they'd say," Yeah, I guess it's humid here too." If I told them it was cold in Japan, they'd say," Yeah, I guess it's cold here too." It never mattered where in the world I lived, or what terrible situation I was enduring, it was always the same at home.

A person can only relate to those things in their own background knowledge. If you never experience the pain another has endured, you will probably never become empathetic to the person's pain. This doesn't mean that if you take a trip around the world, flying first class on

Lufthansa Airlines and staying in the Hyatt Hotel, that you have actually had an international experience. As a matter of fact, you have had the biggest illusion of your life. You should have just saved your money and gone to Disneyland.

Tourists are not treated the same as those foreigners who live and work in a foreign country. Tourists never have to go through the painful experiences of getting proper visas at the immigration office in a foreign country. Tourists never have to live in an apartment complex where nobody likes you because you are from the U.S. Tourists are treated kindly by those who want their money. The nicer they are to you the more money you will spend, and you may return again if they are extremely nice. Those who are not tourists are expected to leave as soon as possible and never return. A foreigner is often asked, "When are you leaving?"

Rationalizing the World

Attempts to rationalize the world and use it for our own benefit are doomed to failure because we cannot possibly know where our benefit lies. I am more empathetic with the possibilities of crossing into the invisible realm than most other humans on earth, but when this vivid possibility is disguised with the glamour of spaceships and alien abductions, my stomach turns. I assume that those playing out alien abductions are crying out to be heard for their true spiritual encounters. I assume they are being infiltrated by an Infinite power that is allowing them to fly closer to the circumference of a Higher Reality. The alien abductions represent a revolutionary period where the masters are coming forward and admitting that there is a virtual reality. There are now respected scholars who are willing to go beyond the Quantum Reality into a possible Higher Reality.

Unfortunately, when I heard researchers, psychiatrists, FBI agents, acclaimed authors and Harvard professors speaking on the paranormal adventures of those who have slipped through cracks in the world, I wasn't the least bit entertained or enlightened. It sounded like a regurgitation of the lectures I heard at Aquarian Conspiracy Conventions twenty years ago.

Those of us who have really experienced culture shock of entering the paranormal experience of visible and invisible realities - that obviously can't be seen by anyone else - have a hard time being excited by a story like this: I was driving my car out of Palm Springs into the Desert. All of a sudden everything disappeared. I was in a time warp. I must have been abducted by aliens. When the lady was asked what the aliens said to her, she replied "We should learn to get along with each other better." Certainly that statement is a nice sentiment.

Gee, I wish all I had to do was drive through Palm Springs to have such an experience. What about those of us who have really been living in the jungle, experiencing things that the world will never believe because of those Harvard professors who have been brainwashing us to not see anything for centuries. How do we know this isn't just another one of Harvard's experiments of lowering our IQ's because we don't have the genes that they believe are so special. There is actually a movie camera being played right through each group's eyes, projecting their reality into the society they live in. And what happens when someone is not in their movie? What happens when a foreigner or an alien comes into the movie that they are projecting?

I had my most eye-opening experience when living and working in Seoul, Korea. Many times when I walked down the sidewalk with plenty of room on both sides, a Korean person would run smack into me as if he couldn't see my body approaching him.

This happened to me so many times that I decided to conduct an experiment to see if I was actually invisible to these people. An older Korean was standing on a corner staring right through me one day. So I walked right up to him and looked in his eyes. It seemed like he was blind. Then I waved my hand in front of his face. He still didn't realize I was there. Then I started speaking Korean to him. At that moment he snapped out of it. He jumped as if to come out of a coma. His eyes refocused on me and his mouth dropped open. Again I said, "Anya ha sayo" - Korean for hello. He then replied with a nod. I was not in his movie projector until I said a word that was in his movie - the Korean word for hello.

This was the first of multitudes of intercultural experiences that proved to me that the physical reality becomes less and less meaningful and real, the more we realize that our language and our behavior and attitudes are simply cultural patterns which are designed differently in each different cultural group. These cultural patterns prove to be a hypnotic device that make people believe they are physical beings living in a physical universe when in reality the Matrix of Illusions can be described more like people are being movie projectors playing whatever movie is placed and developed in their head.

Write in Your Journal

1. Describe a situation when you felt someone was not being empathetic to you.

2. Describe a situation when you may have been totally blind to someone else's experience.

3. How many times have you heard someone tell a story of an experience in a foreign country? Are you sure that person has even been to a foreign country? Can you tell the difference between a storyteller and someone who has actually experienced something? Are you sure? How do you tell the difference between a cultural anthropologist and a dreamer?

Crossing Over

So, how do we finally cross the border from the visible reality to the invisible reality? It happens when we turn off our movie projector and let the Cosmic camera project through us the virtual reality of oneness. The true creation has been here long before the world began projecting all of its imagined movies about who we really are.

Anthropologists took pictures of the hypnotists in India doing magic acts such as climbing up a rope into the sky and disappearing. When they took a picture there was no man there except the one standing on the ground holding the rope. The same hypnotic illusion was performed by the cheru who made the orange tree grow in front of an audience in 45 minutes bearing fruit. But when they tried to eat the fruit the illusion disappeared. But when the old guru who had trained the cheru not to use hypnotic tricks performed the same miracles, there really was a tree and they could eat the oranges. He used no tricks. He was simply aware of accepting those things that eyes can't see and giving thanks that they are. When we believe something is there, it appears. The old guru showed that the only illusion is the belief that we cannot make an orange tree grow before us.

When we see the divinity - it will appear. When we see Christ Light in every face, we gain the power of Divine Light's movie projector beaming through our eyes. It is Divine Light projecting the Christ Light through Man. This is the reality. The man we project with eyes, or with a mortal vision, is a hypnotic illusion.

Write in Your Journal

1. Are you fascinated by magic tricks?

2. Describe the reality that you see when you look at a person through the movie project of Love.

Aren't We Capable of More?

We are all brainwashed to be much less than we actually are. Every time I look at a multiple choice question, I wonder why anyone would want to be trained to think like that. It is to mold our minds into little irrational boxes. Look at this question: Is music 1.) a series of notes 2.) a group of notes 3.) notes organized logically or 4.) something you listen to?

This is extremely common in our education system. Only a moron would want to answer such a question or ask such a question. Our education system creates moral idiots. A teacher who wants to create brilliance in students by seeing the Christ shining through - Divine intelligence - as the true movie being projected is first scolded and then either coerced into conforming or fired. Education demands the promotion of moral idiocy.

The world loves to make us fit into pre-organized formulas. Application forms are my favorite. If your address doesn't fit on the form, you are disqualified. If you don't make your money the same way everyone else does you are disqualified. If you didn't take the same classes as the director of the program, you are disqualified. This doesn't leave any place in our society for growth or individuality does it?

Write in Your Journal

1. Do you believe that multiple choice questions allow you to give the right answer?

2. Do you believe that education has given you the tools that you need to live in the Matrix of Reality?

Levels of Consciousness

People are presently living a several different levels of consciousness or awareness. At a lower level, man is living in a totally physical reality creating contradictions and barriers to any possibility of growing past these physical illusions. Those who are living at a medium level of consciousness are usually grounded in a set of physical illusions about who they are and where they come from.

Those living in a higher realm of consciousness have already realized a breakdown of beliefs in physical realities. These realities may be learned through a visionary state of realizing, believing, creating, dreaming until the invisible becomes almost as real as the physical and visible.

There are so many spiritual and metaphysical believers in the universe today that I believe we are very close to a revolution of very high level of consciousness. Those who are at lower levels are trying to climb into their highest level of understanding. Those who have the greatest barrier to more spiritual growth are those who are quite content with the visionary and creative levels they are now maintaining. Many of those who are consciously ready to receive Nirvana have instead chosen to remain masters of their own spiritual creation, rather than allowing the Cosmic Movie to perform through them.

Those of you who already know you are masters, will easily be able to understand the fine line between the visible and invisible. Others will need to rely more on the physical examples I have given, but no matter how many examples are placed in front of your eyes, you will never grow out of materiality until you believe the invisible is more real than the visible.

I have relied on spiritual healing all of my life. I don't think there was ever a time when I believed any medical theory about the human body. I've been having conversations with Masters all of my life. But, even at a very high level of consciousness, I never achieved complete Oneness until I allowed God's movie to be projected through me.

Write in Your Journal

1. Describe the level of consciousness that you are presently in.

2. What do you need to do to reach your next level?

Culture Shock

A combination of being a cultural anthropologist with an extreme intuition and spiritual sense has opened up realities about the world that are totally invisible to the normal individual.

Culture shock after culture shock of passing from one worldview to another year after year has made me realize that no human picture of what is reality is any more real than another human picture of reality.

Every cultural group in the universe has a certain value and belief structure that forced them into the consciousness level they are presently in. Through a combination of world beliefs, family programming, society programming, educational programming, political programming, media, religious and workplace programming, as well as fitting into their friend's pre-programmed movie of who they are, people become nothing more than a scene in a movie that someone else is playing in their head. When we are able to change the movies playing in our heads and shining through our eyes to conform to the perfection of the Divine Creation as seen through the Creator's eyes, the world will transform to the kingdom of heaven - beginning with transforming diseased bodies into perfect bodies, stressed lives into harmonious lives and war torn countries into peaceful countries.

In order to stop wars, violence, anger and stress in the world and in your life you must begin by raising the vibrations of your entire thought structure and entire body to the level of absolute being. When you become wrapped in the arms of your positive energy that shines from the kingdom of heaven within, you help replace the illusion of the absence of the kingdom of heaven. You then create the virtual reality of Unity Consciousness -pure being extending as all existence in the universe. War cannot exist in this virtual, divine reality.

Write in Your Journal

1. Describe a time in your life that you experienced culture shock. How did this change your thought patterns?

2. Would you prefer to remove one illusion at a time or just step into reality all at once?

Epilog

We must change the movies in our heads from the Quantum Physics of pre-Einstein to the Virtual Reality of Divine Consciousness - the state of consciousness when you allow the pure white light that you can easily keep glowing. This light that shines from inside your pure being holding the kingdom of heaven deep inside illumines the virtual reality of Divine Light's pure Being within you, which can then be lived out from. Holding the kingdom of heaven deep inside illumines virtual reality of God's true perfect creation to beam through your eyes as a movie projector allowing Divine Love's virtual reality movie to play on earth.

Chapter 6

Matrix of Illusions

When we obfuscate the reality of the Divine Matrix with any mortal belief, such as less than perfect health, less than perfect abundance, less than perfect intelligence, or anything other than the perfect manifestation of everything in the Divine Matrix, we have stepped into the Matrix of Illusions. This Matrix is full of illusions, because anything other than the perfect white light cell expressing itself at the speed of light in infinite forms, is only an illusion.

Why do we need to dedicate so many discussions to illusions, instead of just concentrating on reality? Good question. Because 99% of the population is dedicating 99% of their thought and existence to the Matrix of illusions and about 1% or less to the Divine Matrix. How do we know this? On the one extreme, we don't see anyone ascending, or moving mountains, or raising the dead. On the other extreme, we see most people being easily manipulated by whatever controlling group and willingly following them without giving it a second thought.

Write in Your Journal

1. List all of the things that you dedicate your thought to that are not a part of the Divine Matrix.

2. What activities are you doing that manifest the Divine Matrix?

3. How many examples of the Divine Matrix have you seen in your lifetime?

Manifesting the Divine Reality

Yes, there are many spiritual healers out there accomplishing wonderful healings. I am aware of thousands of spiritual healings that have been accomplished at the point in time when doctors finally announced the sure death of a patient, and at that time only were the patient's family willing to give the Divine Matrix a try. I am aware of spiritual healings of people who were shot in the heart, who had their entire brain mutilated, who had complete arms and legs appear in their original perfect condition after being amputated. Yes, all of these things the world has made us think are miracles happen every second of the day because they are not miracles, they are the reality, and anything less than perfect is the illusion.

Why are so few manifesting the desires that are the divine inheritance of those who pray with a true scientific understanding of Divine Reality? If there were only 70% of thought dedicated to the Matrix of illusions, there would be no need for hospitals, if only 50% of thought was out of focus with the Divine Matrix there would be no need for banks, if there were 75% of thought dedicated to the Divine Matrix the government would disappear, and I hope we all know what happens when we return to 100% of the Divine Matrix. The Divine Matrix contains the complete spiritual understanding that allows the original Divine Creation to appear and become manifest in the forms we presently need.

Write in Your Journal

1. Describe the thoughts that you dedicate to the understanding of the Divine Reality. How much of your life is manifested in the Divine Reality? What is keeping you from manifesting more of the Divine Reality?

Removing the Illusions

There are two reasons people are living in a world of illusions instead seeing the divine reality. The first reason is because they want to, and the second reason is they believe that no other existence is possible. Since there are so many modes of error that are sneakily pulling us into the Matrix of Illusions each day, it is wise and necessary to become aware of these modes, and to become aware that these modes are illusions - not reality. The illusions that will be mentioned are all a part of the world's lowered vibrations. Instead of vibrating at the speed of light where we are the mirrored images of the white light cell of all creation, we have first lowered that vibration into a form visible to human eyes. But, which came first - the eyes made mortal or the vision made mortal?

Our eyes are the radiating camera where the Divine Matrix can be radiated into the world. So, it isn't the eyes that are imperfect. It is the mortal visions that have been placed into the eyes through the world's hypnotic trance that is making us see a mortal vision of the Divine Matrix rather than a spiritual vision of the Divine Matrix.

The first step to realigning our vision with the Divine Matrix is the realization of the things that are participating in our hypnotism. In order for a world government to take control of a spiritual government, the people must be transformed into the beliefs of the new system. This is exactly what we do when we create any world organization, system, group or family which are all in fact a culture created by and maintained by a set of beliefs and values. The spiritual beliefs and values have been transformed into world beliefs and values, and then, the world makes us believe these beliefs and values are actually spiritual because they claim these are the same beliefs and values taught in the Bible. Here is the root of much evil.

This is the hypnotic trance that we all signed up for. We all chose to believe that our culture and our government is a reflection of the divine reality. We have all been manipulated to believe that our nation is run by God, and our church reflects Christ's teachings. God's government is the eternal Life Force that we become a part of when we align our thoughts and purpose in life entirely to the divine reflection of all of the divine qualities of Oneness. Did we all miss the fact that the U.S. government has removed the phrase "one nation, under God," from the national pledge of allegiance? Didn't we already separate Church and State? Didn't we already remove all Christian teachings from our schools?

Christ's church is the temple, meaning the body that is allowing the Life Force of Universal energy to maintain, sustain, direct, guide through the essence of one white light cell manifesting at the speed of light the Divine Matrix of Reality. If our government and church were doing these things, there would be no government or church because the fundamental principle of the Divine Matrix is One Universal Life Force all emanating from One White Light cell.

Government and Church are for the purpose of separation into the ones who join this one and the ones who join that one, depending on which one did the best job of manipulating one to believe that their mission is the closest to the real Christ mission on earth. Every church is for the purpose of leading sheep. Those who are not sheep will not find themselves in a church. As long as people are sheep, they will easily be manipulated by the Matrix of Illusions. Those who are no longer sheep are looking for something on a higher plane of understanding. Even those are still seeking and finding some new realization each day. There are many illusions that are blocking the alignment with the Life Force. It is the intent of the following discussions to help those who are no longer sheep to remove 50% of the Matrix of Illusions, and then 75%, and finally return to the White Light Reality of the Kingdom of Heaven.

Write in Your Journal

1. What illusions have you signed up and dedicated yourself to in your lifetime?

2. Are you directed by Divine Mind or your church?

3. Are you motivated by Divine Mind or human values?

4. Are you sure your values are Christ's values? How do you know this?

5. Are you sure that you know the difference between the thoughts of Divine Mind and the thoughts planted in your head by the government and society? How do you know the difference?

The Matrix of Illusions

We have all been molded into the World's Matrix. This matrix is a web created by governments to control the people and to mold their minds to fit into the war program that will allow any government to go to war at any given time in history. The human brain or the mortal mind is the government's tool, which only contains the information the government wishes to have implanted upon it. The mortal mind is only a psychic phenomena - it does not reflect reality. The only place reality will be found is in Spiritual Consciousness or the Matrix of Reality.

Each one of us is bound by gravitational pull, climate, geography and atmosphere only because we are living in the psychic phenomena or Matrix of Illusions planted in our minds so that we may become the puppets of those "chosen few" who have set themselves above the rest of us, put themselves in charge of our money, our minds, our lives, and then created an education system which would keep us under their feet for as long as we succumb to their plan.

When we place our minds in the hands of mortals, we are allowing ourselves to become puppets. When we place our minds in Divine Consciousness, we are allowing ourselves to become individuals - individual reflections of the real Spiritual Consciousness that created us. This is true freedom. In order to remove the psychic phenomena that the human brain places us in we must raise our thinking to the highest activity of consciousness - activity such as envisioning infinite love, infinite being, expanding our vision beyond all human binding forces. As long as we live through the human brain we are locked out of the spiritual reality and locked into a mortal dream that binds us through gravitational forces.

The real translation of "Get thee behind me Satan," is Get thee behind me inhibitor. The inhibitor is the human mind creating binding forces, creating limitations, creating barriers. The education system was created to inhibit our minds. The "chosen few" in charge created a system that would inhibit our minds to believe only our nation is under God, only our country is good, only our race is good, only our beliefs and values are good. This education system has done a great job of brainwashing us all into becoming warmongers. In fact our education is based on the Prussian education system, which was designed solely for the purpose of creating a population who was ready for war.

In order to be set free from the Matrix of Illusions we must begin by demanding Satan (the inhibitor) to be cast behind and to begin to surge forward toward the Matrix of Reality. The Matrix of Illusions has obtained its control through the mortal mind, which is a psychic phenomena. It is very easy to manipulate, hypnotize and brainwash on the psychic plane because this is a plane of unawareness. Many become so comfortable living in the psychic plane that they don't realize that they are dream walking. This dream state is a manipulative control coming from many modes or channels in the world including the government, chemists, pharmacists, doctors, researchers and anyone needing minds that will mold into the their missions of creating warmongers, creating diseases, creating illness and helplessness that will bring those dreamers into their web.

Write in Your Journal

1. What has inhibited you in your lifetime?

2. What is keeping you from stepping out of the dream of mortality?

3. What is keeping you from becoming free from the need for doctors?

4. Do you want to be free from the inhibitor?

Recognizing the Inhibitor

This text will take a general look at how the Matrix of Illusions has become your reality. The modes that are used to bind you to the illusions will be examined and explained. The reader will have a solid idea of how to recognize all of the inhibitors that are presently binding him or her to the earth's gravitational pull and the government's brainwashing of humans who will hate and kill other humans. These inhibitors will all lose their power in our lives as soon as we recognize the modes and channels that are used to inhibit us from expanding our viewpoints, expanding our visions, creating a new reality much larger and closer to our real being of Spiritual Consciousness. The reader will realize that the only reason that the affirmation of Get thee behind me Satan (Inhibitor) has not been claimed toward these modes of erroneous beliefs, is because the Matrix of Illusions has trained us all that these inhibitors are the "good guys" and those who go outside the circle to broaden their minds into a spiritual reality are the "bad guys." We have all been conformed to the Inhibitor's rule through wanting to do the "right thing." This platitude set for us of right and wrong is the first and most powerful tool of all to place our mortal minds into a state of hypnosis to become servants of the world.

Our minds don't want to easily remold around new sets of information given to us about situations we thought we knew about. Our brain doesn't want old information to have to be reformatted and reprogrammed. We would rather spit it out and say, "No, that's not true," or "No, I have never heard that before." How many want to run to the library or internet in order to investigate the claim to see if it is true? Well, if you do that, you'll just find more incorrect information. Much of the information that is made known to us is what the government wants to be made known to us.

Until we learn to do our own research, collecting our own data through conversations, ethnographic observations, comparing stories of people who were actually there, we will never know the truth about anything. The U.S. Admiral, who stepped forward and made a documentary about what actually happened at Pearl Harbor, couldn't tell the truth until he was so close to death that it made no difference. This was also true for the leaders of the Vietnam War. How many other true stories have been taken to the grave? And how long can the government keep us blind to the truth about the Magic Bullet Theory explanation of the coup d'etat of President Kennedy, the reality of the Vietnam War, the truth about the Mid East Crisis, Bin Laden, North Korea, and then we'll examine the medical cures that are banned through the brainwashing of doctors who are not allowed to humanize or recommend vitamins, who can only recommend medicine approved by the government - not governed by the proof of health, but by the proof of killing.

What happens to those who have had their cultural blindfolds removed to the degree where they can see through the lies that have been planted in their heads by the church, the school, the government, the media, the society? Those who open their eyes during a war get a court martial and are shot for being a traitor. Those teachers who open their eyes get fired for refusing to use the textbook and curriculum that is full of lies. The doctor who opens his eyes loses his license for telling a patient the truth about a drug or the benefits of taking vitamins. The mother who wants the truth for her child must remove herself from society and become a home schooling mom.

And those of us who speak a little too loudly about the truth get thrown in jail or put in the funny farm with the other funny people who opened their eyes (of course there are also people there that are in need of help). A friend of mine who was teaching Logic at the same college where I taught communication was removed by the police and fired because he tried to promote freedom of speech in his classroom. A student, who was the son of a local policeman, decided this teacher was a traitor to his country because he was sharing his opinions about the government. The student complained to his father and his father became irate because of his narrow minded narcissistic view of how teachers should only teach the textbook.

So, it has already been shown that it will not be easy to detach our minds from the Matrix of Illusions. It has always been easier to go along, to conform, to be manipulated, or to do whatever the employer says, even if you know you will be hurting others by doing it. It is only hard to leave the Matrix of Illusions if we don't know how to live in Spiritual Consciousness. We can't leave something unless we have somewhere else to go. However, we can't begin to obtain Spiritual Consciousness until we are willing to leave the inhibitors in the mortal mind and go straight to the activity in Consciousness where we remove all inhibitors and go straight to Infinite Possibilities. When we tell the Inhibitors to get lost, we have created a place for Spiritual Consciousness to guide us to a better place.

Write in Your Journal

1. What inhibitors have you always thought were the good guys?

2. What inhibitors have you always thought were the bad guys?

3. Are you willing to speak the truth, or more willing to conform to a lie?

4. Are you ready to take the first step toward infinite possibilities?

Epilog

If you have answered all of the questions and written the answers in your journal, you have taken the first step toward removing the inhibitor. You have made a commitment to step out of the Matrix of Illusions and return into your true reality. When we start seeing illusions for what they really are, we start to make the system crumble. We become the anomalies of the system that was created to control our minds. We become the creators and the producers of our own movies instead of the actors and puppets for someone else's movie. Welcome to the Matrix of Reality.

Chapter 7

Expanding Reality

One of our greatest perceivers, Albert Einstein, when speaking of a subject thought to be literally concrete and figuratively black and white, stated, "As far as the laws of mathematics refer to reality, they are not certain; and as far as they are certain, they do not refer to reality."

Many critical thinkers say that perception begins the very unique human experience and continues influencing our uniqueness throughout our lives. We begin life with stimulation of our senses, thereby becoming aware and interpreting the world around us. We move through life by growing, changing, and sometimes rejecting our perceptual building blocks. Perception refers to the way we receive and translate our experiences - how and what we think about them. For some, plain yogurt is delicious, while for others it is disgusting.

Level of Awareness

Your success or failure, your reactions or fears, your level of emotions towards different phenomena including disease, death, winning or inheriting a pile of money, etc., are indications of your level of awareness - your thoughts and emotions. Your body and mind reflect your level of awareness - your thoughts and feelings toward different situations and elements in the world whether it be to make money or become powerful.

In reality, we mirror or reflect Divine Consciousness. We have the ability and the right to mirror Divine Reality rather than the mortal thoughts that create and imprint the ideas of disease, failure or even the surprise of sudden wealth. As a mirror of Divine Reality there would be no more reaction to an inheritance of a million dollars than the arrival of a beautiful new flower on your rose bush because each of these is a reflection of infinity that is already ours.

When we allow our minds to become the mirrors of Divine Supply, Divine Inheritance and Omnipresent Being, our lives reflect this reality in continuous achievement, advancement, and the ability to rise above the illusion of the mortal dream. Don't let your body (your temple of God) become ordained by false information created to make money for others. That would be reason for God to be a jealous God. That is like selling your body to make money.

There was a time when man sacrificed living beings to a vengeful and jealous god because that was their highest concept. These people reacted to mortal made illusions that we realize as pure stupidity now. There will soon come a day when our present level of reality appears just as ridiculous as prehistoric man's superstitions.

We have all been programmed by the world (education, society, media, family and government) to react in a certain way to the criteria that has been deemed appropriate in each societal or cultural grouping. The buttons that have been programmed into our mental technology causes us to have negative and positive reactions. Each time we react, we program a negative pH balance into our cells and we eventually transform our white light cells into the programmed cells that will mirror the disease, death, war and political hell that the world (matrix of illusions) wants us to be.

We all have the choice to maintain our Divine reflection of white light, where there is no reaction to error (programmed matrix of materiality) or to react to every material illusion placed before us until we are transformed into dust.

It has already been shown that it will not be easy to detach our minds from the Matrix of illusions. It has always been easier to go along, to conform, to be manipulated, or to do whatever the employer says, even if you know you will be hurting others by doing it. It is only hard to leave the Matrix of Illusions if we don't know how to live in Spiritual Consciousness. We can't leave something unless we have somewhere else to go. However, we can't begin to obtain Spiritual Consciousness until we are willing to leave the inhibitors in the mortal mind and go straight to the activity in Consciousness where we remove all inhibitors and go straight to Infinite Possibilities. When we tell the Inhibitors to get lost, we have created a place for Spiritual Consciousness to guide us to a better place.

How do we un-program our minds and bodies? First we must realize that we have been programmed. Next, we need to see how we've been programmed. Then, we need to transplant the Divine Reality back into its original place where the material lies were placed.

Self-Actualization

The origination of materiality started light years ago. The matrix of illusions that we are being transformed into in this life time has come from the government's plan to create un-self actualized people who will be too ignorant to know the difference between a Divine Reality or a bad commercial.

Abraham Maslow has defined self-actualized people as people who feel at one with the world and are pleased with it instead of being outside looking in. The themes that Maslow says these people would experience would include wholeness, perfection, completion, justice, aliveness, richness, simplicity, beauty, goodness, uniqueness, effortlessness, playfulness, truth, self-sufficiency. For a complete understanding of these principles, see Abraham Maslow (1968) in Toward a Psychology of Being.

Abraham Maslow has done extensive work in providing substantial proof that our education system creates people who are not self-actualized. John Taylor Gatto (2001) has stimulated further evidence of Maslow's findings and proven that it was the government's intent to create an education system that would prepare high school graduates to be nothing more than coal miners and servants of the system who are moral idiots (morons). Gatto's evidence provides the foundation for realizing that we have all been scammed. Maslow has shown us how the education system places our mind in a dichotomy, a trance of unawareness, molding minds that will always be looking the wrong way, a nation of clones reflecting the image of a programmed idiot. No wonder Jesus said, "Forgive them for they know not what they do." Most people don't have a clue why they do what they do because their ability to know what they do was eliminated by the school system.

The ironic part of the joke is the fact that everyone with a two-year college education has studied Maslow's Hierarchy of Needs. The education system has handed to us the proof that our education system creates morons by putting Maslow's theory in the textbook. And then the joke plays itself out because the government already programmed anyone with a high school education to never read beyond the textbook. The students study Maslow's Hierarchy of Needs, they pass the test on Maslow's Hierarchy of Needs. They all know that it is an important theory that everyone should know. But, the system makes sure they all miss the point that this formula is showing us about ourselves.

Those who do not research the entire meaning behind Maslow's hierarchy do graduate from college, do get jobs teaching and managing and writing more textbooks. And those same people will reflect the Matrix of Illusions in this lifetime and a few more life times after this one. Those same people will allow their cells to become programmed into dust.

For those of you who are not familiar with Maslow's hierarchy of needs, it simply states that the focus of the lowest evolved person is on survival and food, the more evolved person is on maintaining that level of survival, a little more evolved may become focused on using their work for gratification of lower basic needs or as a response to cultural expectations, and in some cases out of habit or neurotic needs. As a person becomes more evolved on the scale of the Hierarchy of Needs, he or she becomes more and more aware and motivated; and, in some rare cases, he or she becomes self-actualized. However, Maslow says he has only met a couple of self-actualized people in his life.

Maslow has done ample research to prove that the education system is blocking, denying and actually creating mental barriers that deny educated people the very possibility of becoming self-actualized.

There is a very good reason why the government would want to create an education system in which the person who remains in a state of mind far below self-actualized becomes capable of passing tests that promote them as leaders in our military, government (such as IRS, national security, government representatives to other countries, etc.). There is an even better reason why the self-fulfilling prophecy of the IQ that is the indicator of a person who fits perfectly into the mold of becoming saturated with so many trivial facts that they couldn't possibly utilize their minds in a way that would raise others levels of technology, science or education to a higher level of intelligence.

The government of every country is only concerned with creating servants of the system. The U.S. education system emulates in form and purpose that of the Prussian education system's sole purpose of creating nationalists who are prepared to step into a war at any given moment. Substantial evidence of this is provided in great detail with ample proof and verification in John Taylor Gatto's Bible on Education, entitled "The Underground History of American Education" (2001).

The Prussian government succeeded in doing this, the German government succeeded in doing this and the U.S. tested the effectiveness of its system during WWI, II and on the Vietnam draft. The U.S. government assumed that all high school graduates would be perfect draftees because they had created the system to create such non-thinking nationalists. Much to the government's surprise, there was a large group of non-conformists resulting from the insightful visions of hippies and peace loving teenagers of the 60's and 70's.

There were enough self-actualized people available to protest against slavery and war and to continue progress toward a better civilization in spite of the government's attempts to create war clones. The government blamed their failure of total brainwashing a generation into becoming warmongers on the new free thinking methods in education. These methods that were blamed for the Me generation, hippies and other self-actualized beings were removed and replaced with more rigid standards of promoting ignorance in the classroom. Testing was enforced as the tool to make children focus on the small group of facts taken out of context of the reality. Young minds were kept so busy memorizing trivia that they could not possibly grow into a self-actualized culture capable of making decisions such as war is a bad thing. As a matter of fact, the majority of war promoters during the Iraq war came from the church rather than the school. The government found a new way to control the minds that had the greatest potential for self-actualization. According to Maslow's hierarchy of needs, those going to church would be the best candidates for self-actualization.

Write in Your Journal

1. List all of the self-actualize people that you know. Describe their qualities. What makes them self-actualized?

2. Explain why a self-actualized person couldn't possibly choose to fight in an unjustifiable war.

3. Why would Christians want to promote an unjustified war?

Removing the Most Important Teachings

Since the government has always worked hand in hand with the church, even in creating a Bible that would leave out all of Christ's teachings that they knew would interfere with doctrines of the Roman government, they knew once again that they could rely on the church to misinterpret the Bible in order to serve their goals of obtaining power, control and world domination.

I was amazed when a student told me that her church believed that wars were good because the power of God would destroy anyone who did not follow the teachings of Christ. The preacher in this church had taught this student and the rest of the large congregation that it was not only necessary, but good to destroy those who did not believe as they did. This same church contains many military members, had demonstrations of war planes flying over their church as a social activity and passed out flags to the entire community to hail the U.S. military invasion Iraq.

It was already evident to me that I lived in a community of zero self-actualization level. Apparently, the government uses this low level thought of the church to propagate warmongers. This church was receiving grants from the government to promote warmonger thinking. Of course this church is only one of millions receiving grants from the government for activities that will promote nationalization and the type of education that the government wants. What has caused the generous donations toward education in the church? The government knows that self-actualized parents are taking their children out of public schools and doing home schooling. Many of these good-hearted parents do not realize that the immoral training they are protecting their children from in the public school system has been transferred to the church as well. Yes, it is more likely that the son won't get beat up at church as at school, But the same propaganda will be taught, the same brainwashing techniques will be used because the government is supplying the textbooks to the church. And it is the textbook, which was created by the government to replicate the Prussian method of creating soldiers. So, Onward Christian Soldiers, Marching as to War. What a nice song to brainwash children and entire congregations into believing that there must be something very Christ-like about wars - even wars that have absolutely no justification whatsoever.

Write in Your Journal

1. Explain how you will make sure that you are not being brainwashed by propaganda, manipulation or world education.

2. Describe the difference between Divine Knowledge and World Knowledge.

3. How will you make sure you are not eating of the tree of knowledge of good and evil?

Know Thyself

In Japan there are two commonly used words meaning "not included in the group" or "cast out of the group." The words wagamama and ijime are the most feared situations in Japan. If a person is not fitting into a group correctly, the group will ijime him/her until the individual's behavior blends harmoniously back into the group through much humiliation. If a person becomes wagamama, s/he will never get back into his group or any other group in Japan as long as he lives, and has also caused his entire family to never be allowed back in. The behavior that allows a person to enter into a group originally is called "hazukashii" - to be shy, never say an opinion - to always fit in.

As a U.S. teacher living and working right in the middle of group relationships starting from pre-kindergarten through university students, as well as the group behaviors of faculty and staff, I became very familiar with group behaviors that accommodate, scorn and cause suicide or even murder. I witnessed identical behavior among pre-kindergarten children as with high school, university and faculty members.

People from the U.S. are familiar with media anecdotes about the Japanese student that must work so hard to accomplish high scores that s/he sometimes commits suicide when s/he fails. This folktale couldn't be further from the reality, which has been hidden so well from the world's eyes. I will never forget about the Japanese mother who spent five long years pleading with the government and the high school where her son was murdered to admit that her son did not commit suicide. Her son, who was found dead, rolled up inside of a large and heavy wrestling mat at school. The mother stated over and over again, "The wrestling mat is too heavy and large for my son to roll himself up in. Someone had to put him in it and roll him up in the mat. My son was killed" This same boy had several threats made to him over the year. The Japanese high school students who attacked him daily to get money refused to admit they had killed him. The high school teachers, who were as guilty as the students who murdered the child denied that they had actually promoted the situation. The mother could prove the same group stole her son's bicycle and the faculty refused to acknowledge that crime either. There are, on the average, one killing a day (about 360 kids a year) in the Japanese schools - each portrayed as a suicide by the school and the police.

Let me ask the readers if you have ever questioned the reports of the Japanese suicides yourself? How did the media arrange for you to believe that young people would be so courageous or extreme as to end their own lives because their grades might insult their family? There has been an actual conspiracy of the government and media to create an illusion that makes reality invisible both in the U.S. and in Japan. The conspiracy has been to make people in the U.S. believe that the Japanese education is so much better than theirs and that Japanese students work so very hard to become over achievers. Wake-up! This just isn't the true story.

If the U.S. media is working this hard to plant lies in our brains about the Japanese education system, isn't it possible that they are making the situation about the U.S. education system equally invisible to us? What is really driving high school kids to pick up a gun and shoot those students and faculty who have been torturing them and making their lives hell? Isn't it possible that these same children may have ended up dead themselves just like the Japanese children do? And don't we teach our children to fight back and stand up for their rights beginning in kindergarten? And how is a flimsy little seventy pound weakling going to defend himself from the entire senior football team as well as their coach bullying him, punching on him and threatening him every day he goes to school? Where is the evidence that the faculty or administration or parents have taken any steps toward eliminating a wagamama and ijime process in the U.S. school system?

If you never experienced the pain of wagamama when you were a student or a foreigner, you probably can't empathize as easily as I can about the pain these children have endured for centuries in the U.S.

How does Education Prevent Self-Actualization?

What are the elements in education that prevent self-actualization? Since self-actualization requires the ability and desire to see the big picture, to go beyond the little boxes that were created by the schools, religions and cultures, the education system trains children to keep everything in little boxes through categorizing and separating essential elements of subject matter into long lists of meaningless data, which takes all of their available time of their youth to accomplish and then criticizing and punishing them for drawing outside the lines.

The crucial element in becoming a self-actualized person is to become transcendental to all culture - to go beyond culture and to be able to look down from above one's own culture as well as all others without judgment or bias - but just to look at all of the variety.

The school does not allow self-actualization because our education system is based on and enforces nationalism. Nationalism is a biased, one-sided viewpoint of everything in the world. Our education system teaches students to become incapable of seeing another's point of view. Tests showed that college graduates - other than intercultural majors were totally incapable of being empathetic. The U.S. education system creates people who are not capable of empathizing to those in their own culture, society or family. They are even more incapable of seeing any rationality behind any other culture than their own.

What type of school system graduate is needed for a government who wants and needs to create soldiers and national leaders who will continue to overpower, control and demolish other countries. A self-actualized person would not and could not be a part of such a self-demeaning, un-worthwhile cause.

What would be the differences in the outcome of two peoples' lives if one person was a self-actualized person who was non-judgmental of others cultures and could transcend the belief of some cultures being good and others being bad, while the other person had been locked into the narrow, biased, nationalistic viewpoints of the high school text books? The later would be easy to transform into a soldier. The later would also be easily transformed into any diseased case that medical science industry would like to plant in his/her mind. The second person would react with negativity toward anything unlike his narrow minded self. It is living within a controlled dream where someone else is controlling the dream - it is a Matrix of Illusion.

Epilog

Begin looking at every day as part of the movie or myth that you wrote with characters who would fulfill the purpose of whatever great message you wanted to leave on earth or whatever grand achievement you wanted to accomplish on earth. Start seeing the narcissists who attempt to take your identity away as the villains in your story, and those who become the demolished at the hands of the demonic narcissists as the pawns or victims needed to complete the myth you have prepared for the world to audition.

Begin to look at each day as a new adventure full of communication barriers that only you have the key and the magic to show the world how to easily turn in to a victory for yourself and for the future readers of the myths you will leave on earth. When you find yourself written into a part or a dialogue that seems too painful to complete, remember that you are the writer and you are the director. You do not need to be a method actor who intentionally makes him/herself feel pain in order to complete your role. Remember, all of the world is the stage, and you are in control of your movie, as long as you remember to stay in the movie that you wrote instead of getting drug into someone else's movie.

Reference

Gatto, John Taylor (2001). The Underground History of American Education. NY: The Oxford Village Press.

Chapter 8

Real Meaning

Those who share the same personal and cultural background knowledge also share the same vibration of meaning in their language of communication. It is this vibration set within the words that conveys the meaning between two people. If the people believed in Omnipresence of one being there would be the authentic communication of oneness. Within this oneness there would be no verbal arrangement between the two communicators. The vibration would be the vibration of oneness. The communication is a cloud of spiritual meaning enveloping the communicators in their oneness.

Stepping Stones

Every event, situation and relationship in your life is a stepping stone to heaven. We each create our own semiotics of people, events and the language that surrounds these. We each create a semiotics, which can block us out of the vibrations of Divine Mind or totally immerse us in the Kingdom of Heaven. Semiotics became an important

function in my own life to help people understand the
difference in cultural relationships, which has helped
eliminate judgment, hatred and stupidity in my classrooms.
This same semiotics can help remove blindspots in each of
our human relationships in order to help us remove the mask
that keeps us from seeing the master hidden behind the mask
of cultural blindspots.

Write in Your Journal

1. Describe one event in your life that might be blocking your
from the Matrix of Reality.

2. Explain how a misunderstanding of what someone meant
kept your from seeing the master behind the mask.

Mistranslation of the Bible

Socio-linguistics is an art that can help us see the validity
behind the mistranslations of the Bible as well as the need for
the guidance of an Ascended Master - St. Germain - to take
the language to the level of vibrations in order for the
language to survive the disintegration of meaning that the
government undermined. St. Germain was especially
interested in the preservation of harmony on earth and was
always available to assist in important matters such as the
writing of the St. John's version of the Bible.

Write in Your Journal

1. Do you believe government officials have the spiritual
insight to edit a divine revelation such as the Bible?

2. Do you believe the government would think it was in their
best interest to publish a book that would allow people to be
governed by Divine Mind?

3. Do you believe that the government would have more or less control of people who had discovered their Divine rights as the image and likeness of the Divine Creator?

4. Why do you think the Roman government edited out the most important years of Jesus Christ's life from the Bible?

5. Do you believe that the Roman government could remove the Divine power of a book, regardless of how hard they tried?

Transferring Meaning

Language is a means of transferring/sharing meanings between people. What those without an extensive background in cultures and people remains blind to is the fact that language is a creation of the culture, and the true meaning of any words lie deep inside the cultures that they come from. The deep understanding has become so shallow that any religious organization, which is a culture unto itself can rewrite the meaning of the Bible through the small minds of the cultural beliefs existing within its culture rather than through the eternal Divine Mind that originated the meaning.

Write in Your Journal

1. Do you read the Bible as one listening in Oneness or in separation?

2. Choose one word or phrase in the Bible, such as the promise of a perfect kingdom, and dwell on those words in oneness.

3. Choose five more words or phrases in the Bible or any other spiritual doctrine and dwell on it in oneness.

How Deep is the Rabbit Hole?

We've just seen that the rabbit hole is so deep that it could suck us into its illusion of ultimate termination on the very day of our birth - unless the matrix of illusions of your family, friends, and society is exchanged for the Divine Matrix. So, the majority of us are already born firmly tied into the Matrix of Illusions, unless there is something greater, more powerful than the thoughts of our family, friends, and society waiting to free us from the rabbit hole.

Even if we are so lucky as to have a mother such as the one that replaced her stillborn baby with the true divine creation that was meant to be, there is the second set of rabbit traps waiting for us when we enter elementary school.

I perceive John Taylor Gatto as clearly indicating, identifying and documenting in his books on education that all children are sent in to a rabbit hole of misinformation designed to create non-thinking, misinformed, unmotivated, material zombies who are moral idiots designed to work in the coal mines of corporate America. The money/power people of the world have clearly set in place every possible rabbit trap for any human being who dares to let his or her divine intelligence shine through in the classroom. Those who cannot prove they are morally dim witted will be beaten down with the stupid stick until they conform to the social norm of morons who will believe anything the boob tube tells them about what food to eat, what drugs to take, how much smoke to inhale, how to have sex, how to eat worms to redeem your fear factor, how to chose a wife from a brothel of cackling chicks, or how to lose all your money in the stock market.

Do doctors ever diagnose us correctly? Do doctors even give us the best cure? Doctors such as Dr. Lark ,of Women's Health, says doctors rarely tell us the truth or prescribe the best cure (Dr. Susan Lark's Monthly Newsletter). She provides hundreds of examples each month in her newsletters that indicate how doctors actually give out information and drugs that are harmful to patients health - formulas that have already been prove to cause cancer and death, and also deny homeopathic cures that have proven to be much more beneficial and not harmful to women's health. The Life Extension magazine is another source of information implicating the FDA in millions of misdiagnosed illnesses and deaths, and proof that the government has kept drugs that were proven as cures to cancer, gangrene and many other diseases out of the reach of U.S. citizens. The government causes sick U.S. citizens to need to travel to other countries for cures that are badly needed here.

What motivates the society to choose the lies fed to us by education, medical and other government controlled groups? Societal control is manipulated by cultural controls set up through values and belief systems, which are set up through religious and educational groups. We are told what is good and what is bad by our church, and we believe we are good because we do whatever they say to be good. We become so controlled and manipulated by the desire to be good that we forget the commandments thou shall not kill, and blessed are the peacemakers and forgive them for they know not what they do. Instead we decide it is good to kill rather than forgive and it is better to make war than peace. It only takes one sermon at church to get the whole congregation to pull out their machine guns and go shoot innocent men and women in someone else's country that has absolutely nothing to do with them in any way.

We are so brainwashed by our society, our media and our church that we wouldn't stop for one second to consider the fact that we are living in a matrix of illusions where the government can create magic acts of illusions right before our eyes that will make us believe that someone else dropped the bomb, someone else shot the president, someone else made the stocks crash. And we will always be looking the other way when the buildings fall on our heads.

And then Chicken Little says, "The sky is falling; the sky is falling." Yes the sky is falling. We are allowing the matrix of illusions to make our world crumble into utter chaos. We allow the government to make our world crumble into utter chaos. We allow the government to make our unborn babies heart stop beating and if they can't make it stop before it is born they will try to make it stop beating by taking away any reason to want to live in a world run by wolves in sheep's clothing and lined with narcissists waiting to cut your heart and soul out every day at work. This is the nature of the Matrix of Illusions.

More than One Meaning

The Korean Printshop Incident - a True Intercultural Incident

A number of years ago I was a professor at a University in Seoul, Korea. One time I urgently needed to have some printing done at the print shop next to the university for the following day. I was giving a presentation at a communication conference, and I had to have some extensive handouts to hand out. I went to Mr. Lee, the owner and manager of the print shop, and told him I needed to have the handouts copied, collated, and stapled by the next day. He invited me to have a seat and made me some instant coffee. We both sat and had coffee and chatted for a while. Once again, I asked him if he could make the copies by the next morning. He told me that he could. I told him I would be there early the next morning to pick them up. The next morning I took a taxi to the university and went to Mr. Lee's print shop to pick up the handouts. When I got there, Mr. Lee told me that he didn't have them ready. I was disappointed, but I asked him if he could have them done by noon. He said he could do that. I left thinking my problem would be taken care of. When I returned at noon, Mr. Lee informed me that the copies were not ready yet. This time, I became a bit upset and a little red in the face. I asked him directly if he could have them finished by five o'clock so that I would have them for my presentation at six that evening. Mr. Lee assured me they would be done. When I came back at five o'clock, Mr. Lee still had not completed the copies. I became irate, yelled at Mr. Lee, and took the originals. I had to give the presentation without the handout, which made me have to do extensive writing on the blackboard in order to convey my message, and the audience didn't receive the additional detailed information about the topic that was in the handout. End of incident.

Why is it so difficult for someone from the U.S. to understand that Mr. Lee's communication pattern is equally correct, truthful and valid as what the U.S. person has been programmed to believe? And isn't it possible that the U.S. person is equally blind to something that he/she has been programmed to do that actually isn't truthful at all?

The reason it is so difficult to understand Mr. Lee's behavior is because the socio-linguistic function of the verb "yes" in English and the verbal equivalent of "yes" in Korean isn't an equivalent at all. The verb "yes" in English would imply that Mr. Lee has the time to complete the work agreement. The verb "yes" in Korean means that there is a human relationship between Mr. Lee and the U.S. person.

In the English language the verb is placed between the subject and the object. In Korean, Japanese and many Asian languages the verb is placed at the end of the sentence. The languages were created by the people to symbolize the meaning of objects to relationships between people. The Asian languages place the human relationship above the action taking place between the people in the relationships.

It might be easier for the Western mind to understand this semantic relationship if the family arrangement is observed. The relationship of family members remain the same regardless of the actions between them. In most normal family situations a mother continues to love the baby regardless of how many times the baby spills food, empties the cabinets onto the floor, paints pictures on the walls, or needs the diapers changed. The relationship between the mother and baby stays the same, while the action is something considered extemporaneous to the maternal ties.

This strong paternalistic relationship exists in all Confucian oriented relationships. The Confucian philosophy throughout Asia is as strong as any of the Western beliefs such as Darwinism, Freud's philosophy, Christianity or any set of Western philosophies.

Which came first? The people or the language? The people exist and language is a tool and form of expression. Language is used for interaction within the cultural milieu that the group of people created for themselves over time. Each cultural group, which could be any group of people in a certain geographical location, created a set of social rules and the language reflecting the semiotics of that group of people.

Linguistics and Semiotics show that the meaning is not in the language or words - the meaning is negotiated between people, and is tremendously influenced by the perceived relationships between the two people. This meaning is very fluid and changes in each situation. A grammatical arrangement of words may become very fixed through a set of rules. These rules were man-made to take the flexibility of human relationships out of the English language, and created a very sterile fixed meaning that can only be translated through a low context set of rules. This sets up a colder, more inhumane use of language, which allows it to easily be used to hurt people in the court room and elsewhere.

The Ascended Masters have informed us that the Bible was a mistranslation created by cultures that were based on the folklore of passing down information from one mouth to another and by translators who had no comprehension of the Christ Culture which all of the semantic meanings were created from. The culture of the Divine Creation or the

Atlantis Continent was a culture based entirely on the reflection of the One Infinite God Creation where there was only perfection and only Now. There were no words or correlative meanings to anything that was negative, there was no grammatical ability to speak in the past or the future because there was only now. These semantics that are necessary to give the proper meaning to the comments made by Jesus in the Bible did not exist in the minds of those translators who wrote the Bible. As a matter of fact, the real name of Jesus Christ is Issa. The writers of this story didn't even get the name of the start of the movie correct, let alone the lines he spoke in God's movie.

Write in Your Journal

1. Write down all of the cultural beliefs that turned your life into a myth that is not a part of the Divine Matrix.

2. Write down all of the beliefs that were placed in your mind by textbooks that have turned your life into a myth that is not a part of the Divine Matrix.

3. Write down all of the beliefs that might be presently blocking you out of your Divine Reality of Being.

Epilog

Begin looking at every day as part of the movie or myth that you wrote with characters who would fulfill the purpose of whatever great message you wanted to leave on earth or whatever grand achievement you wanted to accomplish on earth. Start seeing the narcissists who attempt to take your identity away as the villains in your story, and those who become the demolished by the demonic narcissists as the pawns or victims needed to complete the myth you have prepared for the world to audition.

Begin to look at each day as a new adventure full of communication barriers that only you have the key and the magic to show the world how to easily turn in to a victory for yourself and for the future readers of the myths you will leave on earth. When you find yourself written into a part or a dialogue that seems too painful to complete, remember that you are the writer and you are the director. Remember, all of the world is the stage, and you are in control of your movie, as long as you remember to stay in the movie that you wrote instead of getting drug into someone else's movie. Make sure that your movie is not getting totally mistranslated like the stories in the Bible. You have the power to communicate in a way that allows your meaning to be understood in any language through the process of authentic communication.

Chapter 9

Love Poison - an Adventure

Allowing Divine Reality to Appear

The only reason that life on earth would appear to be, or turn out to be less than fruitful, or even painful is because we have been trained to look at life through someone else's blueprints instead of the ones that we personally designed for ourselves, for whatever purpose it was that we wanted to fulfill. If we have designed blueprints for some architectural design where we expect to live in a mansion with many rooms and tunnels, but the builder decides to build our home from a blueprint of a dark cave, we are not going to be very happy in our new home. This is exactly what each of us has done to ourselves.

We have each designed a plan, which we wanted to live within and share with those on earth before we left the other side. Yet, when we arrived on earth we became so hypnotized and manipulated by the world, that we each became molded into someone else's blueprints in order to fit in to the world.

The blueprints that we are often drawn into are what I will call the Matrix, or the web of lies designed by the world that we are living in. They are so convincing that they seem to make our original blueprint disappear or become an illusion. The world of lies would like to keep us sound asleep inside the dream of mortal illusions where we can't even remember what our original blueprint was. This is accomplished through an agreement of agencies in the matrix including the government, education, religion, families and all cultural beliefs that hold us in a trance to their governance of our every thought and action.

We will be sharing with you a series of true events that have appeared in our lives as the phenomena needed to complete our own blueprints. The Matrix of Illusions will always make the mind believe that a tragedy is happening, while the Matrix of Reality will show a Divine Event directed for the victory of the Life Force to appear as the guiding and directing force of reality - appearing in whatever form is necessary in that event.

Adventure - Love Poison: an Attempted Murder

This adventure will begin with a tragedy in a 5 Star hotel in Korea. The question to be asked throughout this adventure is who actually had the tragedy. Was it a tragedy for the training consultant in a foreign land? Or is the real tragedy staring the reader right in the face? How many tragedies can you find in this situation? An amateur may only see a few hundred tragedies, while the expert may find millions. And the sad reality that will be learned is how narrow minded many of us actually are and how many choose to remain narrow minded simply because ignorance is bliss.

What this adventure will do is open the eyes of the reader to see that there actually are other points of view than those we find laid upon us by our own tiny societal perspectives. There are other realities beyond our small town newspaper, our small minded education system, our biased ethical standpoints. There is a big element left out of the Westerner's perspective that the Asian cultural web of family ties, relationships, being humans first could actually help a Westerner become more aware of how un-human the present cultural and work perspectives actually are. There is an equally large blindspot in the minds of those who automatically attack someone who is actually trying to protect their best interests, only because their minds are programmed to believe the "outsider" is the enemy.

Regardless of the perspective taken, someone is always right and someone is always wrong until our minds are opened to realize that both sides are equally valid. There will always be someone lurking in the hallways, or listening on the phone, searching for ways to sabotage those who are doing their jobs well or above average. There will always be those who threaten, sabotage, slander, back stab those who do not help them pave a path to success with no effort of their own. We don't care about those people. We care about broadening those minds that have the potential of a future in the global world.

We can begin by asking simple questions about what it takes to have effective interactions in International Business situations. We can look at the foundation of equality that Martin Luther King promoted. We can look at the roots of the Western World's Christian heritage dating back to a Roman empire, using Christianity to promote the strengths of one nation's government.

It is imperative that the reading audience keeps an open mind from the beginning of the story through to the last page of this book in order to rearrange the blindspots in minds that have only been given a very narrow perspective of the realities in this global world. After examining this case from the evidence of the Matrix of Illusions as well as the Matrix of Reality, you will see yourself, people in different cultures and the entire world in a brand new light of awareness and you will begin questioning your own judgments of everything you see and hear in your life, in your business and in the media in order to be sure you are not being blinded by realities that are being forced on you for the convenience of the corporate world and the government to be utilizing your weakness to make money and gain power for themselves.

Write in Your Journal

1. What do you think your original blueprint may have been?

2. How have you rewritten your blueprint?

3. How many times have you rewritten the Matrix of Reality with the Matrix of Illusions.

Answer these questions now, and again when you finish the book.

Writing our Blueprint of Reality

Now we will examine one day in my life and show how this one day may have been the key to rearranging my blueprint until it finally corresponded with the original blueprint written in the Kingdom of Heaven.

A Normal Day or a Tragic End?

Would this be just another day at work, or the end of my life? My assumption as Intercultural Trainer and Consultant at a Joint Venture Hotel in Seoul, Korea was that this day would be the same as any other day. Another cup of coffee, another day of "anya ha sayos" (Korean for "How are you?"), another

day of gathering ethnographic data in the hotel to design
training from - at least the day started out that way. I would
like to share my story about my worst day at work. Let's take a
look at how the day began, the strange turn of events, and the
tragic ending.

How the Day Began

Flagging down a taxi with the palm turned down is the way
most people caught their rides to work in Seoul. Waving at a
taxi or screaming stop might get you run over - or get mud
splashed in your face. So another normal taxi ride to the
hotel it was. Tipping the taxi driver as usual and being
greeted at the front of the hotel continued as normal. The
coffee seemed fine, and everything appeared to be where it
always was.

A Strange Turn of Events

What was different about this day was the nervous behavior of
the hotel personnel, the staff in my classroom in particular,
who met me with very deep bowing and repeating I am sorry,
I am sorry, dozens of times. The nervous shifting of eyes, and
several warnings of "Please be careful." Only days before I had
witnessed a double bookkeeping procedure that was to be
reported to the Western Manager. It wasn't clearly a concern
to me as a consultant, since my function was auditing
communication - not bookkeeping. Which of these two events
would be of more concern to the personnel director and
financial consultants of the hotel - the communication audit
or the financial audit? In a culture where the human
relationships come first, any management strategy that would
be for the purpose of eliminating workers would be a crucial
concern.

Was I being caught in the middle of something that I was
unaware of? Many of the employees at this hotel were

orphans from the Korean War. A person with no family in Korea was like a non-person. The hotel was the only source of family or identity these people had. The personnel director was equivalent to the father. These people had lived and worked in this hotel their entire lives. For the first time in history, this hotel had taken on a Western partnership that would take on 49% of the management. The new Western Manager, who had just begun his job in Korea, had created his prime objective of eliminating problem workers through the process of communication audits and language training. I had arrived at the hotel just in time to help the manager achieve his prime objective.

The Tragic Ending

The strange behavior of bowing deeply and saying "I am sorry" was my first reason to become alert to every move and event from that time on. After going downstairs and having a cup of coffee, my head began to feel very heavy, which was another warning. I also noticed the Korean waiters glancing at me and acting extremely nervous. The cue had been taken that it was time to get out of the hotel as quickly as possible. This was the first thought, since going to the hotel nurse would just be involving one more of the conspirators in the plan. A voice in my head warned me not to go to the nurse's office located in the back alley where there would be no witnesses. So, I made it to the front of the hotel to get a taxi home.

I was not conscious by the time the taxi arrived at my apartment. The next memory was of my husband coming home and me saying to him, "I think I've been poisoned." My husband consulted a pharmacist who confirmed the belief. My husband immediately went to the Western Manager at the hotel to get a letter documenting that the consultant's work was satisfactorily completed, and that she was free to stay in Korea and work for other companies. Since the Western Manager had legal jurisdiction as sponsor at this moment, the immigration officers honored the statement and stamped the passport as legal alien resident.

The Korean Personnel officials from the hotel were only a few moments behind my husband on their way to the immigration office. By the time they had reached the immigration counter where they attempted to have their U.S. consultant (me) kicked out of the country as an illegal alien, their plan had been intercepted by the letter the Western Manager had written explaining the situation. My husband had placed this letter in the hands of the Immigration Office only moments earlier.

Write in Your Journal

1. Pretend you are Sherlock Holmes and collect every piece of evidence you can find leading to the cause of this incident.

2. Note next to each piece of evidence whether you believe you have a solid, factual argument that can be proven in a court, or if your arguments are actually fallacious based on opinion and assumption.

The Aftermath

About ten years later, this incident was repeated at the same Joint Venture Hotel chain in Moscow. The new Western Manager was insisting that financial records be kept and taxes paid according to Western laws. Even though he was warned not to get involved in this, he kept pushing to change the existing record keeping methods established at this hotel until his body was found dead in the street in back of the hotel.

It is interesting that I was being tricked to go to the back door of the hotel where I would walk outside and around the corner to where the nurse's office was located. This would have put me in the exact back street location that the Western body was found in at the same hotel in Moscow. It is also interesting that the Western Manager of the Korean Joint Venture Hotel said he was looking for my body in the Hahn River, and that he put his wife on the next flight out of Korea.

Are these circumstances coincidental, cultural or related to a mafia culture rather than to the local or corporate culture?

Let's look again very closely at every event that happened that day at the hotel in South Korea, as well as all of the surrounding events leading up to the poisoning. Let's look at the cultural variables involved in the entire situation as well as the corporate culture's opposing viewpoints. Let's look at the actual reason the Western Manager in Moscow was murdered in comparison to the reasons the Training Consultant was poisoned. Are these two events related in any way besides the fact that they were at the same hotel chain in two different countries?

Write in Your Journal

1. Why was the result of the manger in the Russian hotel different than the manager in the Korean hotel?

2. What were the similarities and differences between the two situations?

3. Is it possible that the situations were identical and the results would have been identical if Dr. Barnett were not being directed by the Life Force, while the other manager was only listening with human ears and living completely in the Matrix of Illusions?

4. Why do you think the Russian mafia connected with the hotel killed the Western Manager, while the Korean mafia connected with the hotel attempted to kill the Training Consultant rather than the Western Manager?

Epilog

There are many ways the day in the hotel can be analyzed. It can be analyzed from the perspective of a cultural analyst, a criminal analyst, the poor victim's analysis or by those with a judgmental, racist attitude, if we wanted to assume this event took place in the Matrix of Illusions.

Since I know that I was being guided by the Life Force as I kept my mind in the Matrix of Reality, this would be the true reference point for the spiritual analysis of what happened.

However, I do believe that it is good to be aware of all of the assumptions based on lack of cultural awareness that would cause most of the analysis to be unjustified in the Matrix of illusions. Most of the cultural assumptions and criminal assumptions that a Westerner would make would be a result of perceptions that have no relationship to the cultural reality in Korea. It was my own personal journey of analyzing this situation from the insider's point of view and the Westerner's outside point of view that has helped me to line up my own blueprints with those blueprints created on the other side - in the consciousness of the Divine Creator. We have all had our original blueprints drawn over with mortal lies and confusion resulting from events such as these in our lives. The more open minded, broad minded and available to listen in a state of expanded consciousness we become, the more we can see the reality of the illusions placed in front of us.

Chapter 10

Love Poison - an Adventure II

Matrix of Reality vs. Matrix of Illusions

There are many ways that the day I experienced a tragedy in the Korean hotel can be analyzed. It can be analyzed from the perspective of a cultural analyst, a criminal analyst, the poor victim's analysis, or by those with a judgmental, racist attitude. Each of these analysis would be valid if we wanted to assume this event took place in the Matrix of Illusions.

Since I know that I was being guided by the Life Force as I kept my mind in the Matrix of Reality, I can verify that my consciousness remained in the Matrix of Reality throughout this event. Therefore my movie was taking place in God's Movie, and this would be the true reference point for the spiritual analysis of what happened.

Removing Incorrect Cultural Assumptions

First, it is good to be aware of all of the assumptions based on a lack of cultural awareness that would cause most of the analysis to be unjustified in the Matrix of illusions. Most of the cultural assumptions and criminal assumptions that a Westerner would make would be a result of perceptions that have no relationship to the cultural reality in Korea. It was my own personal journey of analyzing this situation from the insider's point of view and the Westerner's outside point of view that has helped me to line up my own blueprints with those blueprints created in the consciousness of the Divine Creator. We have all had our original blueprints drawn over with mortal lies and confusion resulting from events such as these in our lives. The more open minded and available we become to listen in a state of expanded consciousness, the more we can see the reality behind the illusions placed in front of us.

I will provide a short part of the cultural analysis of this situation, but it is more important to focus on the Divine Reality. If you would like to see how the analysis is done in the other forms, I recommend reading How to Understand Our Relationship with Korea (Barnett, 1985) or Intercultural Training in a Multinational Hotel in Korea (Barnett, 1985).

The Divine Reality

How many healings can be found in this one day of my life? So many that I have filled three books talking about them. I have discussed these healings in the form of cultural analysis, which I have found to be a necessary step to the realization of the true healings that are taking place every day of our lives. It is the removal of cultural understanding from our education system and the church, which leaves our minds in a state of oblivion. We may believe that we have no cultural bias or judgment of others, we may believe that we love all of God's children, and yet, how is this possible when we are still supporting unjustified wars? We are still allowing our tax dollars to be spent on the destruction of the lives of God's children. Isn't there another way?

The case being studied on this day of my life included every intercultural phenomena that leads to and results in wars. There were many similar cases at Multinational Corporations in Korea that were managed by Western managers that did result in strikes, walk outs, bombings and murders.

Why was this case different from the other cases in South Korea? Why was this case different from the similar case in Russia, at the same hotel chain? Those who are living in the Matrix of Illusions are living by the sword. Those who are living in the Matrix of Reality are living through the Life Force of Divine Direction, Divine Protection, Divine Supply, and all of the Divine Realities that make those who live in Reality untouchable by material sense.

Yes, I did have intercultural expertise guiding me as well as intuition guiding me. However, I will guarantee you that any other "so-called" intercultural expert would had thought all of their problems were caused by not speaking the language, and they would believe that the American way is the only right way, and they would had died from the poison. It wasn't only my intercultural expertise that guided me. I was also being directed by my intercultural expertise that had been developed through a spiritual guidance in the first place. My entire life has been dedicated to showing that the principles of intercultural understanding are being misused and misunderstood because they are being seen through the veil of ethnocentrism. The first step in leaving the Matrix of Illusions is being able to know the difference between being ethnocentric and being able to expand consciousness into all possible realities.

Write in Your Journal

1. Describe the healings that you can see happening during this day in the hotel.

2. What healings do you see resulting from the relationship between the hotel people and the teacher?

3. What healings do you see resulting from the intercultural insights about this culture?

4. What healings do you see resulting from intuition and guidance?

5. What healings do you see resulting from Divine Direction?

6. What healings do you see resulting from allowing the Life Force to lift me into the Universal Energy where poison could not penetrate by body?

7. What healings do you see resulting from the Divine Timing of my husband?

8. What healings do you see resulting from those remaining in the Matrix of Illusions being unable to touch me?

9. What healings do you see of Abundance of Supply?

10. What healings do you see of Right Place?

Relationships

The essence of my being already realized that all relationships are Divine in nature. I also knew that there was a deep Confucian respect, duty and responsibility built in to the student-teacher relationship in Korea. I had already received many years of guidance from Masters in Korea, providing the guidelines, principles and responsibilities of being a real teacher in the Confucian perspective. The reason that I was an expert at maintaining the true relationship of teacher in Korea is because I had a deep respect for mankind at a spiritual level. Koreans are very intuitive to the reality behind one's beliefs. They could easily perceive my mutual respect of people as spiritual beings as well as intelligent humans. These are the necessary ingredients that help raise our vibrations closer to the white light vibration of reality where the Life Force is able to take over and guide our relationships that are built on a firm foundation of reality.

It was the Life Force guiding the relationships to interact in a way that was giving me insights, intuition and guidance as well as protection against what was prepared for me. I knew there was a level of sincerity when my students said they were sorry, as well as a deeper warning attached to the Mian Hamnida (I am sorry) along with their deep bow. This is the type of interaction that takes place before someone is to receive punishment such as a beating or having one's head sliced off. It was this warning that attached my mind directly to the inner source of Divine Protection that is always available to those in need. This spark of awareness made me aware of many little things going on around me, such as glances, people watching me from all angles, the entire hotel staff seeming to be focused on the same thing, and too many unseen signs to list.

Write in Your Journal

1. Write down your own experiences with Divine Relationships.

Intercultural Insights

The intercultural insights will be discussed in great detail in chapter six. There are numerous intercultural events and perceptions surrounding this event including relationships, evaluations, placement, removal of personnel, the Western Management taking over a Joint Venture partnership. The most important intercultural insight is that all wars and catastrophic events can be avoided when cultural blindspots are removed, when egocentrism is removed, when ethnocentrism is removed, when all finite forms of perceptions are exchanged for infinite insights and perceptions.

Intuition

There is a difference between intercultural perceptions and intuitive perceptions. An intercultural perception would be to learn that you need to hold the palm of your hand down when you wave to a taxi unless you want it to drive on by. A deeper intercultural perception is to learn that the Korean meaning of yes is very different than the U.S. meaning of yes, since in Korean the meaning is based on the human relationship and in the U.S. the meaning is based on a verbal relationship. Getting the intuitive meaning of a verbal and human interaction is something very different. It is very necessary to learn to communicate from gut level feelings in Korea because this is the essence of true human interactions. While there was already a crucial meaning to the I am sorry (Mian Hamnida) coming from so many people all at the same time, there was a intuitive feeling attached to the meaning of these words that could be felt at a gut level. Intuition is a divine interaction between people, which is very commonly used in Korea. The more we learn to sense things intuitively, the more we know what is really going on around us.

Write in Your Journal

1. Write down your own experiences with Divine Intuitions.

Guidance

Since the everyday tip for my services was a fancy cup of Expresso Coffee, decorated artistically with whipped cream and sometimes liquors, I knew this would be the vehicle used if there was a crime being committed here. That thought came to me immediately after I had taken one small sip of my coffee and my head immediately took a whirl. This was just one more piece of Divine Direction that warned me to leave immediately. I was given two direct forms of guidance. One was a direct message to not go to the nurse's office. The second message was to get in a taxi as soon as possible.

Write in Your Journal

1. Write down your own experiences with Divine Guidance.

Direction

I was receiving Divine Direction to leave the hotel as soon as possible. I was receiving a warning to not even consider going to the nurses office, because that is exactly where they thought I would go, and I received direction to give directions to my home before I could no longer think clearly enough to do so. That was the last thing I remember that evening. The Life Force obviously placed my direction in the hands of the Taxi driver after that.

Write in Your Journal

1. Write down your own experiences with Divine Direction.

Life Force Protection

Everything that happened during this day was in the form of Life Force Protection. This type of protection and guidance doesn't appear unless the mind has prepared room for it to enter in. I prayed daily for God's guidance. I prepared my mind to become a channel for Divine Direction every morning when I woke up. I left the events of my life in the hands of my spiritual guides, my ascended masters, the Christ Light and the Life Force every day of my life. While living in countries where people do not speak my language, I rely completely on Divine Protection every step of the way. I rely on protection when I get on a bus or on an airplane. I rely on protection from anyone trying to deceive, manipulate or malpractice me every moment of every day. It is necessary to raise our vibrations to the white light energy to be able to stay in touch with the Life Force protection. The detailed steps for doing so can be found in the Quantum Journey Online Courses or books.

Write in Your Journal

1. Write down your own experiences with Divine Protection.

Untouched by the Matrix of Illusions

We become untouched by the matrix of illusions when we raise our vibrations above the level of mortal sense. When we keep our minds stayed on the Divine Reality, on Divine Consciousness, on Intuitive Reasoning, listening constantly for direction and guidance other than that coming from material sense. We must keep our minds clear from any cloudy sense of hypnotism that will pull us into the material dream of things where we get confused and do all of the things those in the Matrix of Illusions would want us to do. I knew the thought of the mortal in a destructive mode would expect me to be on their same level of awareness. This normal material person would of course think they should go to a nurse when they feel a little dizzy or sick. This is exactly what they expected me to do. I knew I could be untouched by their plan by staying in the plan of Divine Direction.

Write in Your Journal

1. Write down your own experiences of being untouched by the Matrix of Illusions.

Timing

When we are lifted by the Life Force into the speed of light of Universal Energy our speed of light timing cannot be touched by mortal plans. The direction that came to me and my husband through the Divine sense of Time, which directed my husband to go to the Western Manager at the perfect time and to arrive at the immigration office at the perfect time. The Western Manager was in the perfect state of mind to write the exact letter that was needed because he had just been informed of my disappearance and knew my life was in danger. Even his wife had already started to pack her belongings and was headed for the next flight out of town because they knew there was trouble brewing. My husband arrived at the immigration office only ten minutes before the personnel director who had every intention of making me an illegal alien if he had gotten to the counter first. The timing was even more perfect because the immigration officers could see that these personnel officers were attempting to cause trouble with a criminal motive.

Write in Your Journal

1. Write down your own experiences with Divine Time.

Supply

Divine supply appeared in many forms after this day. My husband and I had become stars of a national T.V. program, which offered the highest pay of any available job. I was immediately offered another prestigious position as account executive for several major Multinational Joint Ventures who were entering the Korean market. This position offered a very nice apartment in a prestigious area and a good salary. The company was also willing to take care of the hefty payoffs that were required at the immigration office after the criminals that tried to kill me continued to pay off the immigration office to cause trouble for me. This event also ended in cultural perception levels that have never been achieved before by any experts in the field, and many publications utilizing the event for countless explanations of intercultural events.

Write in Your Journal

1. Write down your own experiences with Divine Supply.

Right Place

We are always in our right place when we listen for Divine Guidance. It was the right place for me to have the job at the hotel. It was the right place for me to come to work that day. I was in the right place for everything to happen exactly as it did because I was under the protection and guidance and direction of the Life Force. It was even right place to be poisoned because this was the greatest healing of my lifetime. It was a powerful healing resulting from being in the Matrix of Reality rather than in the Matrix of Illusions when it happened. I was protected by the White Light Cell that I was created of and sustained by - the speed of light energy that cannot be touched by the human matrix of illusions. Poison itself is an illusion because it would have to be something other than the Life Force, and anything other than the Life Force is an illusion.

Write in Your Journal

1. Write down your own experiences with Divine Insights.

Epilog

The greatest healing and protective influence in our lives is in knowing who we really are. When we know that we are the White Light Reality living in the Divine Creation where we are performing God's movie for those who temporarily left the stage, we can not be touched by the influences of anyone who is living in the Matrix of Illusions and attempting to drag us off stage and into their movie. We become the director and the producer of our movie and we make the illusions of those trying to perform a different movie evaporate from the world's camera. We do this be projecting the movie of Perfect and Now. There is only the reality of perfection and the only time is now. There is nothing happening before now that could cause anything to happen to us in the now. There is nothing imperfect in God's movie that could cause anything imperfect to occur. We must turn all parts of our movie into the Divine Reality.

Chapter 11

Love Poison - an Adventure III

Korean Matrix of Illusions

Let's look again very closely at every event that happened that
day at the hotel in South Korea, as well as all of the
surrounding events leading up to the poisoning. Let's look at
the cultural variables involved in the entire situation as well as
the corporate culture's opposing viewpoints. Let's look at the
actual reason the Western Manager in Moscow was murdered
in comparison to the reasons the Training Consultant was
poisoned. Are these two events related in any way besides the
fact that they were at the same hotel chain in two different
countries?

A Brief Synopsis #1:

Why Koreans would want the Training Consultant removed
dead or alive.

As an Intercultural Training Consultant, I was making observations of all chains of communication in the hotel. The information that I obtained provided proof that the problems in this hotel were not coming from language differences between staff and guests. The problems were coming from cultural differences in perception, including differences in the level of respect found in the language used according to relationships in the Confucian mapping of things. Staff members were also using imperative commands with guests because this is how these meanings translate from their own language. It was found that the training needed was intercultural rather than linguistic.

The Western Manager's mission was to remove 20% of the Korean hotel staff and base his removals on language ability to communicate well with guests. While it was my mission to remove the problem through assessment and training, it was the Western Management's mission to remove staff and save money.

The Western viewpoint of the situation was to use a low context method of evaluation in a culture based on high context relationships. The people working at this hotel had been there since birth, practically, because they were all orphans from the Korean War. The Joint Venture Hotel was the hotel that provided a home and employment for them. Because of the Korean societal requirement of needing relationships based on family connections, these people had no relationships. A Korean who is both an orphan and may have had a foreign parent because they were results of rape during the war has no place in the Korean society according to Confucian relationships. This particular hotel was probably the only place in Korea that these people would be allowed to work. The Western Management part of the Joint Venture was taking over management at that time, and the Koreans may have seen me as the key factor in destroying their entire world.

The hotel personnel officials were directly involved. One reason would be because all personnel are hired because of their human relationships. In this case the personnel director was like the father to these orphans. There was also an element of mafia in this hotel that didn't like their financial information revealed through my investigations.

The pharmacist said the poison was only available in China, and it was illegal in Korea. So, obviously it was obtained through the illegal channels that only the mafia could employ or through the black market. This raises the question of the hotel in both South Korea and Moscow of an international mafia chain having an underlying control beyond the actual local culture.

Even though there was a strong cultural reason for people to be very angry, my students treated me like their good friend and they knew I was on their side.

The mafia may have found out that I knew about their double bookkeeping, even though I never said anything about it. It is also possible that the Training Consultant was merely a decoy for the Western Manager, who may have been doing things that were questionable or dangerous. This would be the explanation that would align the incidents in Moscow and in South Korea at the same hotel chain to the mafia culture more than the local culture.

Write in Your Journal

1. According to the Matrix of Illusions, what would be your assumptions about the above situation.

2. What cultural blindspots may be causing you to misunderstand the situation?

Looking Through a Microscope

Every event that took place in this hotel needs to be re-examined through a cultural microscope, including everything from why Koreans were overly anxious to say I'm sorry every day, but in a mode of panic on the day of the event, to how evaluations are done differently in America and Korea, to the differences in the meanings of human relationships, to the responsibilities of managers over employees, to basic principles of management in Korea and America, to why a female Training Consultant would be chosen to place the blame and poison, instead of a male Western Manager. These are only a few of situational and cultural variables involved in the thick web of the cultural matrix that must be unmasked in order to come to an understanding that allows this training consultant as well as all those who do work in any type of Multinational Management to live with the "is-ness" of the situation based on the cultures and their values as they exist and will continue to exist. I certainly don't hold any grudges or special fears towards Koreans or towards this hotel chain. I have a very thorough understanding that removes all judgment and guides me all human interactions - regardless of the nation the interactions take place in. This is what I would like the reader to gain from this examination of the tragic day in the hotel.

Write in Your Journal

1. What things may you have automatically assumed to be true about the situation without beginning to unmask all of the pieces of the puzzle?

2. What cultural values do you presently have that may make it impossible for you to view the situation empathetically?

Asian I'm Sorry

Let's start at the very beginning with a simple I'm sorry. A person easily says, "I'm sorry" more than thirty times a day in many Asian countries. It is used in telephone conversations or when you go into an office to speak with someone. You say, "I'm sorry" before saying almost anything to anyone about anything. It's also used before you say "just a moment." It has many uses. It's also used in the same way we say, "Excuse me."

The use of "I'm sorry" is considered one of the most polite ways to interrupt another's routine. The idea is to always cause the smallest wave possible when interacting with others in a group.

Write in Your Journal

1. What is your automatic reaction to a group of people who say they are sorry to you constantly?

2. Do you think you say you are sorry often enough?

Sensing Beyond Words

The individual's unconscious identity with their own cultural values is the root of most international business problems. U.S. organizations most often assume themselves blameless in matters of nationalism. The western management was not and is not taking responsibility for expanding their own awareness of intercultural values or the corporate culture of the partner corporations.

In the Joint Venture Hotel event, the western management was controlling the Koreans by withholding communication and information and the Koreans were reacting in a similar manner, which both cultures saw as a necessity of survival.

The explanation for differences in values rests on the assumption that the problems facing each culture, though basically the same, can be expected to differ in intensity and timing. The goal-oriented western management may have a hard time rationalizing the differences in timing of the Korean employee because Korea is not a goal-oriented society. The Koreans are only interested in "being in becoming," as their goal. This western concept of speedy technological advancement does not correspond with the Korean idea of this same concept.

The Korean worker in the fast moving metropolis of Seoul does indeed move quickly and work long hours. But, the goals of completing work and perfecting the work done do not exist in the Korean mind, unless the completion has to do with a relationship.

Write in Your Journal

1. What would be the possible problems between two groups of people with a different perception of time?

2. How do you feel when people withhold important information from you?

3. Describe some situations when you felt it was necessary to withhold information from someone.

The Question of Timing

Many Asians look at time as a process of eternity. What really matters is how life can be made natural and enjoyable each day. If one is pressed by time where is the quality of life?

Cultures that view time in a cyclical, elastic and open-ended fashion also tend to be more group-oriented, stressing the development or preservation of relationships over task accomplishment. Economic success does not guarantee a comfortable social position over time, members of these culture are rarely single minded, and they will pay as much attention to personal matters as professional ones.

Confucianism teaches Asians to look at time as a process of eternity. What really matters is how life can be made natural and enjoyable each day. If one is pressed by time where is the quality of life? According to Confucian cultural values the highest reward in life is the spiritual enrichment and serenity are received from the contemplation and living out of one's living environment. Time is valuable when it is used to achieve this ultimate reward; time is flexible and repeatable regardless of how much present day business wants to go against it.

In the Asian point of view, timing and planning must remain open ended and adaptable, especially because relationships have their own predictable requirements. Schedules must be flexible to leave time for a social meeting. Relationships are a form of social capital owned by business people and associated with the companies they run.

The U.S. culture's meanings involved with communication and doing one's job correctly in this hotel are quite different than the South Korean's meanings, including the polite "I'm sorry," intuitive meanings, and the high context sense of time. The U.S. culture bases meanings on the low context premise that human relations in the work place should be handled like mathematical formulas. What the Korean culture considers a non-human culture is based on things other than the human nature of emotions, feelings, moment-by-moment interactions and intuitions. There is just a lot of non-human, un-feeling, calculated ideas about statistics, economics, budgets, and anything to save-a-buck mentality in the U.S. management system that is incomprehensible to cultures based on human relationships.

These different principles and ethics concerning the high context nature of the relationship of human beings are taken very seriously in South Korea - especially in the workplace. A company has a paternalistic relationship with its workers. The South Korean company has a lifetime obligation to its workers set through Confucian dyadic relationship principles. This is a drastically different concept than the U.S. company that thinks nothing of rifting hundreds of loyal employees at a week's notice. The question to be asked here is, "Why can the Korean company afford to provide sustainable employment that isn't discontinued at any economic ripple, while the U.S. company has no feeling of responsibility toward the worker's feelings, life disruptions or future survival?" Maybe this is a key to understanding the desperate measures taken by the Korean hotel. Maybe a partnership that is not serving the Confucian principles that Korean values are based on, and not considering the well-being of employees, that are to the Korean as family is to the U.S. person, would cause a reaction equal to any human's fight for survival.

Write in Your Journal

1. Imagine viewing time as a process of eternity. How would you readjust your life to this eternity of time?

2. Imagine working in an environment that valued the well-being of employees. Would you be willing to give up this work environment?

Evaluations

This Training Consultant was hired for the specific purpose of providing evaluations to the Western Management that provide proof of which employees should be rifted. The evaluations were to be based on English ability. While I was trying to provide proof to the Western Manager and to the Korean Personnel Director that the communication needed to be viewed as communication rather than English ability, the Western Manager was only looking for a premise to remove employees without considering the premise I had presented that customer complaints were not stemming from a lack of English language, but from a difference in cultural concepts. The Korean Personnel Director had a different evaluation system based on his own relationships with the employees of the hotel. The employees that he had rated as having the highest English ability couldn't even carry on a two sentence conversation with me, while the employees that spoke in an almost native fluency were not given high scores by the Personnel Director. The evaluation scores were based entirely on relationships rather than ability. It seemed to me that this Personnel Director had more reason to want to get rid of me than anyone else in the hotel because he saw himself as the person who was responsible for maintaining the life long relationships that had already been permanently established in this hotel, even if these relationships had nothing to do with communication abilities.

Again, you may be asking yourself, would someone actually attempt to poison or kill someone over a difference in evaluations? The differences in the meanings of evaluations in South Korea and in the U.S. are so vastly different that it may seem incomprehensible for this to be this important to a Westerner.

Now, the question of rifting employees in a South Korean company simply because they do not speak English at a fluent level. First of all, the customers at the hotel spoke many languages besides English, and the majority spoke Korean. Was the premise of evaluating employees for language ability even a legitimate criteria?

Write in Your Journal

1. Can you explain how a relationship would be more important than one's ability to speak English? Remember, only about 5% of the clients staying at this hotel spoke English.

Other Points to Consider

1. Korea is a high context culture. America is a low context culture. Korea is based on relationships. The U.S. is based on rules, policies and economic success.

2. Koreans would never fire employees for economic reasons. The relationships between employee/ employer is paternalistic in Korea. The only reason for separation is lack of loyalty.

3. Human Resource Director's test scores of English level didn't match the information I had on employees' English level.

4. Western Manager wanted to eliminate 20% of Korean employees based on who had the lowest scores on English ability.

5. It was found that Korean managers had the lowest level of English ability.

6. One waiter argued with his supervisor and could never work in Korea again.

7. Personnel were orphans from Korean War and had no relationships in Korea.

8. Organizational Communication Problem Solver reported poisoned at the Hotel. Husband finds Dr. Barnett unconscious in apartment when he returns home.

9. American manager at Westin Hotel in Moscow was found dead, shot three times, in alley behind hotel. The Westerner had made several attempts to make the Russians comply with Western accounting procedures. He had been warned several times not to make the accounting procedures known.

10. Love poison is an illegal drug that was used hundreds of years ago by wives to kill the "little wife" in Korea. It has not been allowed into Korea for over one hundred years. It could only be obtained from China through illegal means. Someone would have to be very powerful (like international mafia-to get it into Korea).

11. When Dr. Barnett was taken to a pharmacist, she was diagnosed as being poisoned with love poison.

12. Dr. Barnett had been warned by a friend who was in charge of security for the President of South Korea that the person in charge of security at this hotel was very powerful and dangerous.

13. One day a Korean female approached me and told me that I should be careful because I was in danger.

14. There were several Korean women found murdered who were wearing red dresses. I was told that only prostitutes wore red in Korea.

15. A little wife was the woman who would have a man's child if his wife couldn't have a son. The wife sometimes murdered the little wife once the little wife's function was completed.

16. I was required to teach the head accountant of the hotel English in addition to my regular work at the hotel. This English teaching was simply a benefit to the accountant who was one of the main people in deciding all policies at the Hotel. When I learned that it was not included in my contract to teach this accountant, I refused to continue teaching him without extra pay.

19. The hotel had a bomb threat one month earlier when the U.S. Secretary of Defense was staying there. A secret passage way was discovered in and out of the hotel, only known to national security.

20. Mr. Barnett got the Western Manager to write a letter saying Dr. Barnett's work had been successfully completed and she was free to find work else where in Korea.

21. Mr. Barnett immediately took that letter to the immigration office to get Dr. Barnett's passport stamped as a legal alien resident spouse.

22. Personnel, Human Resource Directors and other administrators were also on their way to the immigration office to have Dr. Barnett arrested as an illegal alien because she was missing from work for two days.

23. The American Manager said he was about to send out a search party. He thought my body might show up in the Hahn River, along with several other
women's bodies.

24. The Western Manager's wife bought a one way ticket out of Korea that same morning.

25. An English teacher from the U.S. who had been dating a Japanese man when she was working in Japan moved to Korea and found a Korean boyfriend. The
English teacher was found murdered in her apartment. This happened during the same month that Dr. Barnett was poisoned.

Write in Your Journal

1. Think of yourself as Sherlock Holmes, and you need to solve the mystery of why the Communication Consultant was poisoned and who did it. Examine all of the possibilities listed above, and draw conclusions based on what you know about the culture, the environment and all relationships involved.

Epilog

The hotel situation shows that it is an individual's unconscious identity with their cultural values that are found at the root of most international business problems. It seems that U.S. organizations often assume themselves blameless in matters that concern their own culture as well as another's set of values and viewpoints. This was the case in every Multinational Management situation studied. The western management was not taking responsibility for expanding their own awareness of intercultural values or the corporate culture of the partner corporations.

From the spiritual side, when a person is continuously living on a mystical spiritual plane of consciousness where they are constantly reminded of the omnipresence of God, their gears shift up to the feeling of Oneness with the Higher Self who is able to see so clearly that they seem to be floating above the situation and guided as if to be seeing all dangers and solutions in a flash. This level of consciousness lifts a person beyond the astral, the mental, the magic, and into the highest spiritual level obtainable. This oneness with the Life Force is the Highest Selfhood obtainable. This oneness can only be obtained if one is continuously seeking to be the mirror image of the Life Force by reflecting all of the Divine Qualities. One of the Divine Qualities is the ability to only see the spiritual selfhood in all man. The element that protected me from any seeming power of the poison was my true belief that there was something very special and spiritual about the people in this hotel, and my belief that I had returned to a spiritual and mystical place that I had been in a prior lifetime. It was this connection to the past, the present and the future and the astral projection above and beyond the entire physical environment that lifted my body beyond the effects of the poison because I refused to believe that there was any evil in these people that could want to harm me.

I maintained a very deep respect that I had obtained from studying this culture so deeply combined with a very deep intuitive sense that I had remaining from centuries before. I am sure that I was in Korea in at least two previous lives. The first time I was in Korea either as a second wife who carried a baby for another Korean woman or as a geisha girl who was used as a second wife. The second time I was in Korea, I was a Shaman Healer who helped a second wife to survive her destiny. I also have many memories of dragons and soldiers and a feeling of being surrounded and protected as if I had been a queen or a goddess of some type. However, this vision could also be symbolic of the place of the teacher of the Rulers in Korea. I was lucky enough to experience the honor of being a professor at Korean universities and a trainer for many leaders in South Korea, which allowed me to experience this feeling of honor once again in my life.

Chapter 12

Quantum Odyssey

Creating God's Movie

The expansion of consciousness helps material concepts begin to disappear, and this expansion makes room for spiritual discernment. An unfolding of new realities takes place, leading those on a spiritual journey closer and closer to spiritual reality. Each time a new cultural reality is presented to a person's consciousness it causes them to experience the culture shock that allows them to see that each culture is just another set of illusions that have been planted in people's minds. As we eliminate the movies of the world from the mind, we make room for God's movie to appear in our minds.

The World's Movie

The World's Movie contains scenes where people get hypnotized into the mortal dream. The scenes show how they are hypnotized into believing that all of the material concepts, diseases, and theories placed in their heads are real.

After people become hypnotized by the World's Movies, they create their own movies in their heads and play them out as if they were real. These movies are actually a Matrix of Illusions.

Scene after scene of the world's movies that we create in our heads, or lives, are not the reality of our true Authentic Self. The secret of becoming free from these cult-like dreams or lies is to return ourselves to the One True Movie, which is God's movie. This movie existed as the only real movie billions of years before the world 's movie began. In God's movie we are co-stars with our Angels, our Masters, our Ascended Masters and our Prophets, who have all remained in the Divine Creation from the beginning. If we have the ability to remove ourselves from God's movie, we also have the ability to return to that Divine Creation at any time. We each have the ability to reconstruct that Divine Creation as a result of aligning our minds with Divine Mind.

We are the producers of the Lunar Visions movie channel where we keep God's movie playing day and night. Our movie started as professors and corporate trainers working in many countries in every part of the world. While communicating with the host people of each culture that we lived and worked in, we concentrated on the art of Authentic Communication to uncover the Authentic Power in people all over the world. This Spiritual Art allowed us to escape hundreds of tragedies and to live peacefully among the host people and to help resolve international problems between corporations and to give spiritual guidance to families living abroad experiencing many levels of culture shock and cultural adaptation problems.

Aligning our Spiritual Reality

Culture shock and cultural tragedies forced us to realign our realities over and over again with the only stabilizing force there is - spiritual reality. Once you become aligned with one set of realities or culture you become an alien in all other cultures. We have learned to live on this earth as aliens who only connect through the Authentic Power of the Spiritual being that is inside all Universal Beings.

Our mystical experience has led us to expand our visions of reality far beyond what the human eye can see. Our 25 year journey included exploring the cultures of Russia, Turkey, Cyprus, Korea, Puerto Rico, Taiwan, Italy, Switzerland and Japan to lead us into our final Quantum Odyssey, where we were able to realize our presence in all planets and universes as the speed of light Oneness with our Life Force. Living among so many belief groups on earth including Shaman, Muslim, Buddhist, Confucian, Taoist, Shinto, as well as many varieties of Christian groups, helped to expand and connect visions of one reality back to before the world began. This is the point in time where all visions become one reality of the Divine Creation that existed before the material world was created through the Matrix of Illusions. This is the point in time where all Divine Light and Divine Love shine forth through all the eyes connecting us with those who have gone before and those we have passed many times in our lifetime. We can learn the spiritual truths that help us dissolve all cultural realities into Oneness. We can learn the spiritual truths which will help us become one with Eternal Life from those who are living in different cultural realities, virtual realities and those who are living on different planes of consciousness.

Our personal Odyssey began one night in Beppu, Japan as we were divinely awakened to receive a spiritual message in the middle of the night. This is when our spiritual journey began. By the time the sun rose in the little town of Beppu, the first song on the Trilogy Album was finished. The first song was "War," and the lyrics began to tell the story of how we must each arrive in a state of consciousness where there is No More War. The piece begins with the sound of machine guns, the male vocalist repeats over and over the message that it is time for wars to end, and the song ends with the sweet angelic voice reminding us all that "We are made of love, we are made in love, we are love, why not love, why not love, why not love?"

It was this song, directly influenced by our journey in Japan for six years, that began the movie we have been writing for the past ten years. Our time in Japan awakened us to many facts and possibilities that we didn't know existed in the world. We didn't know that when we announced that we were Christians that we would be scorned as the "bad guys" in World War II, who were responsible for the death of thousands of innocent lives. We didn't know that everything we did and said for the years we spent in Japan would be judged as a bomb dropping Christian.

One of the subjects that we were required to teach at a Japanese University was U.S. Cultural Studies. We used this study of the U.S. culture to help our students learn that there is actually much more to Christianity than dropping The Bomb on Hiroshima and Nagasaki. It was this one small bit of information about Christians dropping a bomb on Hiroshima that was placed in all of the Japanese high school textbooks that cast a spell of misunderstanding about Christianity on all of Japan. Fortunately, there were a few men that actually fought in the war that saw this misfortune in an entirely different light.

Regardless of how one goes about rationalizing war, the fact remains that it was the U.S. military who did bomb Nagasaki and Hiroshima, and neither city contained military support since the entire Japanese Navy and Air Force had already been completely destroyed. These cities were simply housing for innocent women, children and grandparents. The U.S. insisted that the only way to stop the war was to kill innocent women, children and grandparents by dropping atomic weapons on two major civilian cities. This is exactly what the U.S. military did. And since the U.S. military was made up of Christian soldiers, this would verify the statement in the

Japanese textbooks that say Christians are people who kill innocent women, children and grandparents.

Write in Your Journal

1. Write your version of what makes a war right or wrong.

2. Find proof in any of the master's teachings that killing is ever a God given activity.

3. Write down how you would explain to someone who knows nothing about Christianity why Christians would bomb with atomic weapons hundreds of thousands of innocent people.

Explaining the Unexplainable

There are already dozens of statues, ceremonies, protests, peace talks, etc. attempting to cure the pain on both sides of this international flame. The approach that we decided to take was to focus on teaching what Christ actually taught and what the God Christ referred to actually is. We were intercultural experts who knew we could not utilize anything in the American culture to repaint the ugly picture left in these people's minds. We had to approach the problem from their point of view. We had to paint a picture of God that they could understand.

We approached the creation of our music through a constant prayer for world peace, and as a result, this healing could be felt in the music. We wanted the music to tell a story and to contain the quality of instantaneous healing that can be felt, understood and realized when standing in the Oneness of God's presence.

We were as successful as we could possibly be. When our Japanese friends heard the music, they immediately saw it as their own. The first remark from every listener was this is our music, this music is about us, this is who we are. This is exactly what we wanted to hear. In our mission of intercultural understanding, we wanted to paint our highest understanding of God, God's Omnipresence, God's glory, God's Healing presence, God's Love in the music. We wanted the presence of God to be felt when he music was heard. We wanted all who heard our music to know that God's presence is universal. We wanted these people to know that our God is their God and there is only one God who loves everyone. What greater proof of One Mind governing all could there be?

We had been living in a culture consisting of thousands of gods. There was a god on each block guarding territories - there were gods of fire, gods of wind, gods for any purpose that one could imagine. Most of these gods were gods to be feared. Now, there was an image of the one Life Force of goodness made available to people who had the possibility of a God who created man in His image and likeness removed from them through that intolerable act of cruelty.

The Movie

The song "War" was the beginning of the movie that we had been directed to create. We wrote many scripts for the movie that year. The movie was originally to focus around a war journalist from New York who was sent to write an article about the conflict of an international war. The journalist was immediately guided by an angel in the disguise of a little boy. The angel directed the journalist into a cave where masters were bringing those wounded and killed in the war in for healing. The spiritual healing that was taking place in the cave is portrayed through the 3D sound in the music of angelic voices directing healing from the walls of the cave.

The journalist returned to New York insisting that he write a story about the healing going on in the war rather than the violence. The editor would not allow his story to be published, so the journalist ended up returning to the war zone and learning from the masters to heal. His girlfriend, who was a nurse in the war, gets shot and dies, and the journalist is able to heal her through the guidance of the masters.

After completing the script and the music, learning everything there is to know about music production and movie production, including becoming involved in other productions (including the hilarious 3D animations Thumb Wars and ThumbTanic). We also learned that any producer that would back us would demand that we change the entire essence, meaning and reason for doing the movie in the first place, yet we received the angel message once again to make God's movie.

We were sure at this point that the meaning of movie must be something entirely different from what was going on in Hollywood because we knew that we would not be directed to this city of confusion by an angel. As we were walking on the beaches of Dana Point one day, the meaning of movie became translated. We needed to start living in God's movie instead of the movie that was being created for us by our family, our society and our world. We started listening moment by moment for direction to stay in God's movie, to know what God's movie is, and to radiate the Life Force as a result of our understanding.

Write in Your Journal

1. If you received an angel message directing you to make God's movie, what would you do?

Making God's Movie

You have begun your own Quantum Odyssey where you will wander through all of the experiences in your life, use those experiences to guide you as you listen for God's direction to stay in the Quantum Reality of your White Light perfection and power. Begin to look at each day as a movie in itself. Begin to look at each moment as the Now Zone where Eternity takes place.

The Quantum Journey Courses have provided a background in reality. This reality check was necessary before you continue your journey into exploring all of the things in your life that have been blocking you from your Quantum Journey into the Virtual Realm where God's movie is playing.

This journey will help to examine all of the times that we have each chosen to be in someone else's movie. Our mothers, our families, our education, our society and our government will be our biggest stumbling blocks and our greatest charges toward finding reality and returning to our spiritual Mother's womb, where God's movie is playing.

We spend most of our time on earth in our mother's movie. We spend the next largest amount of time in the minister of education's movie, and we spend the rest of our time in our nation's government's movie. These are just a few elements of the Matrix of Illusions that keep our minds stayed on something entirely opposite from God.

Write in Your Journal

1. Write down examples of when you see yourself as being projected from your mother's eyes rather than your own.

2. Write down examples of when you see yourself as being projected from your eyes rather than as a white light creation of the Life Force.

Chapter 13

Mindshifts

Our minds are constantly being reprogrammed by the matrix of illusions. In order to remain awake and alert to the world's manipulative forces, it is helpful to change continents frequently and learn to see things from a different perspective frequently. I am not speaking of traveling for pleasure's sake. I am talking about really living in different cultures, with entirely different value structures, life styles, languages, family structures, etc. This is what helps keep the mind flexible and fluid. This is what makes us see from another's point of view. This is what helps us keep from becoming judgmental of anything that is unlike the mental mapping the present matrix is forcing upon us. We receive our wisdom that allows us to rise above the trite formulas and theories that come from textbooks into the reality of experience with true meaning when we travel to foreign lands and meet masters from every culture.

After living on several different continents among dozens of diverse cultures, we have had the opportunity to go through culture shock over twenty times. The shifting of consciousness resulting for these mind shifts have raised our consciousness to a level where we can see things that people who stay in one culture all of their lives will never be able to perceive. We've been teaching the subjects of intercultural communication and intercultural encounters for over twenty years and we've witnessed those who remain incapable of freeing their minds from their present reality even after they have a new set of information given them to that should broaden their perspectives. People from the U.S. often have a difficult time accepting a new reality of what other cultural groups perceive as reality - as do people from most other cultures.

It has occurred to us that culture shock might be the first step necessary in perceiving realities of other levels of consciousness or insights beyond the second or third level of insight. A person has to actually go through the incredible mind shifts that take place when someone adjusts their entire philosophy of being before they can believe there is a reality beyond their own. A person must adapt their values and beliefs to fit into an entirely different culture, other than their original one, at least three times in their life before they can begin to comprehend the reality of other levels of consciousness that are surrounding their own level of consciousness.

We've met so few people in our international journeys that have even been able to adjust their mindset to the new culture they are living in, that we have found that it is very difficult for people to change their mindsets without such an experience. We come from a culture and a world that has had the ability to empathize with others removed from our consciousness. This is all part of the Matrix of Illusions that has been established on earth by the inhibitors to keep us from learning to cross over to another culture, let alone another dimension.

Our professional background in the examination of cultures of the world and how these cultures create blindspots (a phenomena which can not be seen or understood by the other cultures or persons involved) has been used in problem solving for Multinational Corporations to eliminate unseen phenomena causing international companies to lose millions of dollars a month. We also use this expertise in corporate training as well as university and community classrooms to find out what it is that keeps adults from realizing their true potential, as well as the multitudes of viewpoints that should be considered before a narrow minded belief is formed about any phenomena. We also use our backgrounds in the cultural matrix to guide clients in their spiritual journey in spiritual consultations and healing.

The cultural phenomena which prevents us from seeing that which is actually in front of us is the cultural blindspot where a certain piece of information has been left out because of our lack of experience or exposure to groups outside of our existing cultural matrix. There was already a great movie, which explained this phenomena perfectly - The Matrix. The movie portrayed how we have plugged ourselves into the mortal socket of human dreams totally manipulated by our government, our education, and society, forcing us into a deep sleep where we become the puppets of our culture. The star of the show reminded us that we must unplug the mortal sockets, take the red pill to see the cultural blindspots and then envision the unreality of the whole human control phenomena - until it ceases to exist in our minds. At that moment, the quadrillion volts of electrical energy will be transmitted, and we become white light.

We most often get mental blocks because there is one piece of crucial information missing from our research or our chemistry formula, physics formula or spiritual understanding. Sometimes the mental block changes into the belief that the truth has already been found and there is no need for further study or research. Our entire life has been in pursuit of answers to questions that we didn't believe were clearly or truthfully answered by other researchers, other religious beliefs or other educational beliefs.

We have been digging for the truth and fighting with liars in the educational field to allow students to examine all viewpoints outside of the one-sided textbooks all of my life. All one needs to do is take a step outside of the cultural matrix that locks us in through the lies in our textbooks, our society, the media, our families, or what ever the vehicle of the blindspot is in order to see that what we think of as facts are merely a smoke screen that makes us nationalistic, prejudice, conceited and unwilling to learn from those outside of our cultural matrix.

Why is it important to become free from the Matrix of Illusions? There are millions of reasons but three certainly stand out: (1) we cannot know true freedom as an individual until we do, (2) we cannot truly follow our own spiritual path and know and live from Divine Reality until we do, and (3) we cannot even begin to speak of a relative world peace among nations until this happens with a significant number of the world's population.

Write in Your Journal

1. Describe some possible blindspots that might exist in your present reality.

2. Consider and describe any of the lies that may have been planted in your mind through the cultural matrix.

3. Consider and describe any of the lies that may have been planted in your mind through the lies in textbooks and media in the society.

4. Explain how you will begin to remove yourself from the matrix of lies.

Mental mapping

Very few people are capable of escaping the mental mapping that they are locked into. Most people are living within a panoramic worldview that has been projected onto their brains, which they, in turn, are projecting out in front of them as their worldview. The majority of people from the U.S. that travel abroad think all people are the same as they are. They even think people from other countries like them because they live within the commercial virtual reality of the tourist vacation package.

Write in Your Journal

1. What is the culture shock that breaks down the blindspots caused by the matrix of illusions programmed on to one's brain?

Culture Shock

When someone goes over to the other side - or moves into a new country with an entirely new set of cultural maps frozen into the brain, there is a period of pain, shock readjustment, and sometimes deep depression. Everything seems wrong while this shift is taking place. The people seem immoral, corrupt, liars and all of the rules of good and bad change. If the person stays in the new country long enough, he/she can actually readjust part of the mental mapping if he/she chooses to open his/her mind to the possibility that the new set of rules is just as valid as the one back home.

This adjustment is more likely to occur if the person has had some type of intercultural training, education in cultural anthropology or falls in love with someone in the new culture. The optimal cross over happens when all three of these cushions soften the shock of switching illusions. Those who do not have any preparation for the cultural journey sometimes fall into depression, anger and hatred of the people in the country. Sometimes this shock wears off just in time to re-enter the original country. Only weeks after the returnee arrives, he/she realizes that all of the things that were hated in the culture from which he/she is returning were in his/her home country all along as well. However, he/she couldn't see these things before because of the Matrix of Illusions he/she had been molded into. It is like the guy who buys the used car. While he is being mesmerized by the used car dealer about what a great car he is about to buy and what a great deal he is going to get, he is seeing what the used car dealer is creating in his mind. However, when he gets home and finds out the car has had the odometer set back, the rings are bad and the transmission is about to fall out, he realizes that his car isn't so wonderful after all.

For those lucky few who spend their lives moving from one culture to another every few years, this phenomena of culture shock reoccurs during every cultural change. The blindspots in the brain become weaker and weaker and the mind becomes less judgmental of the variety of concepts engaged by many cultures. The matrix begins to lose control of the mind and an individual can start seeing both sides simultaneously. When the mind reaches its height of awareness where it realizes the cultural experiences were merely illusions placed inside of groups of people, it has the chance to be totally free of all of the world's motives of control, manipulation and illusive hypnosis.

Write in Your Journal

1. Describe any cultural blindspots that you have broken through which resulted in culture shock of a new reality.

2. Describe the culture shock you went through when you were a teenager trying live within the cultural boundaries of your parents?

All of you who have raised a child can recite the formulas that you collected to raise your child "correctly" according to some social scale. Some of you used formulas from your church, others from top child psychologists and others from groups that you joined to exchange information. Some formulas may have promoted a total control schedule of training preparing the child to read the encyclopedia and speak three languages by age four. Others may have chosen the freedom formula of no control, which helped establish the me generation.

Whatever formula you chose as a parent, you were programming your child's mind into some preordained mental mapping that fits into the cultural groups that you belong to. The child is being trained moment by moment to understand what is good and what is bad according to the parents self created rules, the family rules, the society rules and the cultural rules of the group the family is a part of.

After the parents finish programming the child, the kindergarten teacher and the children at school begin to mold and shape the child's mind into a new cultural mapping. Again the child is trained to know what is good and what is bad according to cultural rules. The teachers have also been pre-programmed to teach exactly what the society and government wants placed into the child's mind. The child's mind is also shaped by the T.V. programs watched, by the children's groups attended, and by all children that the child comes in contact with at school. The programming becomes more controlling as the child starts up the stream of pre-programmed textbooks that teach the formulas, history, geography and folk stories that the cultural group has agreed on, while being totally controlled by the government's rule and budgets.

This same mental, cultural and societal mapping continues through elementary school and high school. People living in cites, states and countries agree on most things because they have all had a similar mapping. The variations of individual mappings comes from the variety of friends, the parents discussions on guidance and religious beliefs that have been accepted as well as individual choices about how enthusiastically an individual studies at school, partakes in church activities and beliefs, pursues social activities or becomes involved with friends who form cliques, take drugs or skip school.

There is no doubt that each person is an individual depending on all of the variations of the mental mappings. However, each societal group is forced into agreeing on the same basic principles, rules, attitudes, behaviors, and have been programmed by the same government ordained education system. This sort of mapping is so strong that when a new set of cultural beliefs are introduced to a person, the person will automatically react negatively because the new culture doesn't match that which has been programmed into the person as the correct behavior, communication patterns or family behaviors.

Family Culture

What happens if one tries to break free from their family's culture? This culture shock paradigm shift takes place at least three times in everyone's life - once at age 12 when the child shifts from the pineal gland to the thyroid gland for direction. This shift in consciousness often results in the hormonal shift causing the teenager to go girl crazy or boy crazy. It also causes a generation gap between the parents and child. While the child is under the control of the pineal gland, he is still living in the heavenly domain and has little trouble following the parent's guidance. The shift to the thyroid gland is the return from heaven to earth. The child begins the life of mortality. No wonder it is the most painful time of life. It causes culture shock between parent and child because all of the mental mapping rules that have been so carefully programmed into the child over the first 12 years seem to get erased and rearranged.

Culture shock happens in the family culture when the mother becomes the mother-in-law, a new woman replaces the son's mother (or the mother has to train the new wife - depending upon the culture) and all of the rules change again. This culture shock sometimes results in angry reactions, a fight for control of their child into the hands of another person. This conflict grows when grandchildren enter the picture and all of the family cultural variables are rearranged again. Those with no aptitude for broadening consciousness to new realities will have the danger of culture shock to the degree of family breakups, divorce and even complete family abandonment.

Cultural Mythology

I learned to use the culture's own mythology to learn more about the people I lived among and it helped them grow in understanding about themselves. If mythology is used for the purpose of helping us see something in ourselves that we didn't see before, that is good. I prefer to base my teachings on things that have actually happened in my lifetime and things that have happened in your lifetime that you may or may not yet be aware of. As aliens on a new planet, we must utilize every cultural myth in order to help make us aware of things that we have not yet experienced and things that we are already experiencing, but we are not yet aware of.

Begin looking at every day as part of the movie or myth that you wrote with characters who would fulfill the purpose of whatever great message you wanted to leave on earth or whatever grand achievement you wanted to accomplish on earth. Start seeing the narcissists who attempt to take your identity away as the villains in your story, and those who become demolished by the demonic narcissists as the pawns or victims needed to complete the myth you have prepared for the world to audition.

Begin to look at each day as a new adventure full of communication barriers that only you have the key and the magic to show the world how to easily turn into a victory for yourself and for the future readers of the myths you will leave on earth. When you find yourself written into a part or a dialogue that seems too painful to complete, remember that you are the writer and you are the director. You do not need to be a method actor what intentionally makes himself feel pain in order to complete your role. Remember, all of the world is the stage, and you are in control of your movie, as long as you remember to stay in the movie that you wrote instead of getting drug into someone else's movie. This can be done because there is a Divine Reality, which exists outside of the swirl of the matrixes of illusions, that grounds us, so the movie we make keeps us on our Spiritual Journey because we are constantly learning and growing from our interaction within the mythology of the Matrices.

Write in Your Journal

1. Spend one week watching another person every day during the same hour of the day. Each day write in your journal what you see that person doing. It is often most interesting to choose a person whom you think you know quite well. You will learn how little you actually knew about that person.

2. Now, look at your journal notes and decide if this person has any idea of whose movie they are in. Do you think this person is fulfilling the self-actualized blueprint that they originally wrote for themselves? Why not?

3. Spend one week watching yourself every day during the same hour of the day. What did you notice about yourself that you didn't realize before?

4. Spend one week writing down everything that annoys you and makes you unhappy and unfulfilled.

5. At the end of the week look at your journal and decide how to remove those things from your life.

Epilog

Using the virtual reality vision of morphing through the liquid door of consciousness makes it easier to push out unwanted illusions without having to open and close the doors of the mind, which, when opened, allows other unwanted sources to enter in. The more we realize that we a part of a culture which utilizes specific meanings and relationships for the purpose of being controlled by a government that believes that this is their highest conception of the world as God formed it, the more we become free to realize that this is only a movie created by a government which is not God's movie. We each have the Divine Right to stand in the Divine Consciousness where God's movie is playing. We have the choice to stay in a man made movie or to step back into the Divine Creation.

Chapter 14

Culture Shock

We have spent about twenty years traveling around the world. Each country that we have lived in has helped us gain new and broader insights into spiritual reality because each time someone enters a new reality they go through culture shock. Culture shock is a shock to the system about the new realities that appear that didn't exist in their memory or background knowledge before that time. Along with culture shock comes the ability to see things in the last cultural reality that they couldn't see before. So since we went through culture shock about twenty times, we have accumulated layer upon layer of new realities that those who stayed at home cannot conceive of. Yes, this makes it very difficult to return home because it is more like landing on the moon.

Our expertise includes Intercultural Communication, Cultural Anthropology, Intercultural Psychology and the utilization of this background knowledge into problem solving and developing training for Multinational Corporations. This means we have studied in great depth the differences in cultures and the differences in meanings of language and all elements within the culture, and are able to utilize these differences to create new understandings between and among people.

After living and moving between Korea and Hawaii, Korea and California, moving from Korea to California and then to Turkey, and then moving from Turkey to Cyprus, and from Cyprus to Boston and Boston to Sacramento and from Sacramento to San Jose, California and then to Puerto Rico, and back to San Jose only to immediately move to Japan and finally back to California again, we had experienced the culture shock that causes the mind to see many new realities that didn't seem to previously exist. We experienced culture shock upon culture shock until we could finally see through any cultural illusion placed before us without hesitation. Our intercultural experiences were strengthened by working with the Brazilian culture in Boston, working with Italians, Swiss, Norwegians, Germans and other Europeans in Santa Clara, California, working with the Vietnamese culture in Sunnyvale, and again with many Asian and Spanish speaking cultures in San Jose, as well as spending a great deal of time with the Taiwanese and Chinese as well as the Japanese when we lived in Japan. Our growth through culture shock had only just begun when we realized that our own families and neighbors couldn't see any of the realities that we now knew existed.

Japanese Culture Shock

After all of the accumulated background knowledge of all of the peculiar possibilities that exist in the world, we thought Japan was so peaceful and simple that it seemed boring at first. This was before we got to know people more personally and found out what was really on their minds. We learned over a short period of time that the Japanese were still very angry with the Christians who dropped The Bomb on Nagasaki and Hiroshima. We learned that all high school textbooks contain a summary of WWII as Christians dropping

The Bomb on Japan and killing thousands of innocent women, children and grandparents.

This was the greatest shock on my system to date. It was this culture shock that set the Lunar Visions movie into production. We learned two other very important traits of the Japanese people that inspired our music. First of all, most Japanese are Shinto and Buddhist and a few are Christian. The majority of Japanese believe that there are gods in each geographical religion. There are gods, or kamis, watching over each specific city block, each rural block, each area of the home, functions of nature such as fires and earthquakes, and even the affairs of the household, education and business. Each of these gods, or kamis, punishes for wrong doing, and they are not loving, forgiving gods. Japanese fear the god of fire and the god of earthquakes and are very careful not to upset them in fear that they will start a fire or earthquake. They are also fearful of dead ancestors who visit very frequently and cause chaos when things aren't kept as they were. We learned that the Japanese in our area thought they had made their ancestors angry by allowing foreigners to live in their area. This dislike of foreigners also related back to the bombing of Hiroshima and Nagasaki.

The other trait of Japanese people is their ability to become so intuitive that they seem like mind readers. They base their daily actions on gut level feelings and intuition that guides them.

It became our mission to create a visual image of the infinity the omnipresence of the One Divine Creator that is the God Christ spoke of as well as the God of the entire universe within universe within universe. We wanted to re-create the vision of all Divine Qualities and their infinity in a musical form that would help these people understand who we all actually are.

When we performed our music in Japan we received the response that they believed that our music was Japanese music and they called it Kokoro music. Kokoro means the combination of mind and heart. The Japanese people that heard our music felt that they wanted a God that this music represented.

Write in Your Journal

1. Think of a time you may have experienced culture shock. This could be a time when you did visit another country, or a time when you moved to a new city, changed to a new school, found a new group of friends or simply discovered that something that you believed wasn't actually true. Write in your journal your experience with this culture shock and how this situation may have changed your visions and your vibrations.

Creating Music that goes Beyond Culture

We felt that we had created a music that goes beyond the barriers of any cultural belief to restore the original Divine Creation in the minds of all people. We continued our music making mission in the Fujino Art Resort near Tokyo, Japan, and we were told by many music producers that we needed to create a visual component - a video to go with our music.

In Japan we didn't need to use words. The high context, visionary, intuitive nature of the Japanese could understand our music even without speaking English. However, when we came to the U.S., each time we played our music, we found there were two groups of listeners - one group who declared they could see the Divine Creation manifested through our music, and another group who couldn't even hear the music or could hear the instruments and refused to believe that there was a voice in the music. They would insist that there was something the matter with the CD they purchased or that their tape recorder was broken. They truly could not hear the music. They were entirely deaf to the white light reality.

We found we had a bigger problem to solve in the U.S. than in Japan when it came to showing people the white light vision of Omnipotent Mind, Omnipotent Love and Universal Consciousness. We found there were more barriers preventing the opening of consciousness in a culture based on the low context nature of things than a culture based on the high context nature of things.

We learned that our listening audiences wanted a clear and detailed explanation of our music and wanted to be told the story that goes with the music. We thought that we should actually create a movie at first, but we later realized that we only needed to explain our movie to others and to help others to write their own movies. We found that the most valuable thing we had learned was learning how to find God's movie and to stay in God's movie. We needed to reject the man-made movie that the society was placing on us and return to the white light movie of the Divine Creation.

Write in Your Journal

1. Discuss how you will begin to describe your own movie that was written in your blueprint and how you will line up your vibrations with your movie within Divine Creation.

Cultural Blindspots

We are mostly blind to the things closest to us, so we cannot describe the culture we live inside. We are trapped in a Matrix where the realities painted on our minds are only our own. There are different levels of cultural blindness. Those who have a desire to make an attempt to become empathetic to others viewpoints have a better chance of removing their blinders than those who are just content knowing what they know. There are hundreds of levels of cultural blindspots. A cultural blindspot cannot be totally removed until a person goes through some type of culture shock, which is like a jolt that wakes them up to a new reality that they couldn't see before. The producers of the movie The Matrix did a good job of showing us how the probes attached to our brain must be yanked out before the new reality can be seen. The movie also shows that it takes quite an electric shock to wake some one up.

We also make the choice to be a master or a puppet every day of our life. If we chose to be ruled by the world's lies about our health, our supply, or energy level, our age, who our creator is and our true purpose for being here, we have chosen to be puppets for someone else's creation. We become the pawns of those waiting to sell us pills, cigarettes and a place in the cemetery.

The most common form of culture shock is the difference of perspectives that must be interfaced when living in a new country. Sometimes the combination of different food, different life styles and a set of ethics and morals that seem extremely wrong from ones own religious viewpoint are enough to push one over the edge. The person entering the culture of a new country is having their realities and values challenged by a different set of realities and values. Values are something that are so deeply set inside a persons heart and soul that it would take a doctor's knife to cut these values out of a persons heart.

This drive for understanding why people do the things they do has driven me to undertake a career in sociology and anthropology allowing me to understand the means and the mode of all groups of people - including my own family, which has more peculiarities than all other cultures in the world.

It is actually this pursuit of cultural anthropology and sociology that has given me the strength to forgive others for the rejection I receive, and it is the spiritual drive that draws me to search for the spiritual vastness of reality rather than the human forms buried deep beneath the earth. It is the spiritual reality that provides the insights and guidance to help others see how all mankind can live in harmony, while the cultural pursuits make me aware of all of the reasons it would make it seemingly impossible to get along with others who have philosophies, ideologies and religions that contradict our own.

Write in Your Journal

1. Brainstorm on all the cultural blindspots that may be blinding you from God's movie. Write about these in your journal.

2. Describe your present values and beliefs and begin to examine where these came from.

3. Write in your journal all of the values and beliefs in your life that you are sure are a reflection of God's movie and not your culture's movie.

4. Describe the themes in your life that seem to be the dominating themes projected in your present movie.

5. Use the virtual reality vision of morphing through the liquid door of consciousness. Now push out unwanted illusions from your consciousness. Do not allow other unwanted sources to enter in.

6. Write in your journal what you have chosen to remove from your movie. What have you chosen to make sure does not enter in?

Epilog

Cultures are interesting, beautiful, colorful, intriguing, fascinating, and sometimes have ugly and grotesque parts (but not usually very many parts like that). Cultures come about through hundreds or even thousands of years of organic development within a certain group of people. However cultures are viewed, they are always human-made. They are massive sets of concepts woven together to create a certain view of reality. They are not reality itself, but are a view of what is thought to be "real." One "reality" is no more real than the next, for they are all just sets of human-made concepts. They are like "Dream Worlds" created for us to live by. And until we learn that our Dream World is not the only one in existence, we are asleep in our Dream World interpreting everyone's thoughts and actions by our own personal and unique version of our collective yet individual Dream.

Chapter 15

Divine Mission

Who We Really Are

My fellow aliens, we were all sent to this earth with a divine
mission. We must all try to remember what that mission was,
and who we really are. We must learn how this world will try
to reprogram us to believe that we are one of them, when our
reason for coming here was to show them that they are
actually one of us. We were the first and the last. We were the
divine creation. We had our being as the speed of light before
we slowed down our vibrations to appear as a mortal form to
teach others of their reality.

We have created a man-made world separate from God's
kingdom. Every good interaction, bad interaction, tragedy or
triumph we have here on earth is part of the program created
within man's world. God is not giving us these tragedies or
guideposts; we are giving them to ourselves.

Those of us who have watched the The Matrix movies may
have realized that this movie actually portrays the simulation

of this mind control we have locked ourselves into. Like in the movie, we are living within a program of the material world that is making us believe that the world has power over us and controls our actions and thoughts. We must prove, as Neo proved in the movie, that this program of materiality actually has no power over us. The only action that is necessary to win any battle is the action of Love. When Neo began seeing the nothingness of the Matrix, the Universal Energy took over and the world's movie stopped playing. When we allow the Life Force to take over, we put Love's Movie into action.

We are Love's movie. We are the Divine Creation. We were created in the image and likeness of the Divine Creator. We were created through the movie lens of Love. The reason we are here is to perform Love's movie by allowing the Creative Life Force to shine into our consciousness, emanate through us as White Light and radiate out from us as Divine Love.

Aliens on Earth

During my stay here on earth, I have seen myself develop both an intellectual understanding of the people's environment, as well as an emotional and physical understanding of the human environment. The intellectual side of my observations has brought about a continual thirst to learn all I can about living in various different cultural groups on the planet earth. This is a very peculiar phenomena on earth because each different group seems to hate each other, and consider themselves superior to the other group. This is so different than the way it is on our Real Planet.

The real purpose of our brotherhood of man on the other side was to have all share harmoniously our many varied forms and different ways of perceiving the good that is all around us. Here on earth, it seems like they prefer to look for the bad in each other. I have been utilizing this adventure called culture shock to try to experience this phenomena of making the mind shift into different cultural realities without being shocked by the difference in variables.

Each of us has chosen a set of themes that we wrote into our blueprint (our movie) before we began lowering your vibrations of white light to return to planet earth. Please try to remember what the blueprint, that you prepared to accomplish on earth, contained. I will share with you my blueprint and show you how I went about completing the plan I designed. My intellectual side has had a continual thirst to learn all I can about living in various different cultural groups on the planet earth.

The pain involved in trying to make these earth people see that all cultures have the same Godlike qualities as their own in various forms, colors and varieties, is enormous. The people have become programmed into a matrix of illusions where they cannot see anything outside of the little box they live in, inside their minds. The reason people do not have the inability to un-mold their minds from their present reality that they are accepting into a new reality, of what other cultural groups perceive as reality is the lack of empathy training during the entire education process.

It has occurred to me that this might be the first step necessary in perceiving realities of other levels of consciousness or insights beyond the second or third level of insight. I believe that a person has to actually go through the incredible mind shifts that take place when someone adjusts their entire philosophy of being, and to adapt their values and beliefs to fit into an entirely different culture, other than their original one, at least three times in their life before they could begin to comprehend the reality of other levels of consciousness surrounding their own level of consciousness. In order for someone to become empathetic of another's reality they must walk at least a hundred miles in their shoes.

There are many excellent points that I agree with in the earth's literature which helped me grow in the understanding of my path, but I will definitely admit that there is also something I disagree with in every piece of literature that I've ever read. I always listen to God when I'm reading or listening more than I listen to the author of the words. When the words line up with what God is telling me the message is conveying, then I agree with the words that I read. When I get a clear message from God telling me the opposite is true from what I'm reading, then I don't agree with the author. Each piece of literature that I've been directed to read has come to me at the exact time that God wanted it to come to me. There have been some books that I read at a time when they meant nothing to me at all and then later on they had a significant meaning. Other books have seemed trite and unimportant during the first reading and have infuriated me at a later time because of some piece of truth I had learned that would prove the author is a phony intentionally trying to mislead God's children.

I'd like to turn the quest around for all future mythological characters in their quests for knowledge, adventures and ultimate end goal of death. I'd like you to consider the possibility that the theme of reincarnation could be replaced by the theme of each of us writing the blueprint of our lives before we come to earth. And those who remember the story they have written on the other side can successfully, with continuous guidance and protection of spirit guides, angels and God's hand fulfill life as a self-actualized person.

The ability to look at the isness of everything can be developed through the realization that the reality in back of everything we see is God's white light. We are seeing a lowered frequency of white light through mortal eyes, but the reality that we all have the ability to see, is God's infinity of White Light. It is the constant desire and prayer to become at One with our Divine Source, our Divine Creator which puts into motion the Yin and the Yang that directs us to what we need to know. The Divine Principle of Alignment is Universal, the knowledge of Divine Principle is Infinite, the Frequency needed for alignment is the Speed of Light or White Light. The mind that is not built on a firm foundation is easily manipulated by the good and the bad - neither of which are the Divine. The Divine Creation is here. We are standing right in the middle of it. We are the Divine Creation. We are the White Light Frequency. We are the mirror images of our Divine Creator. It is our charges of good and bad that will keep us from seeing our reality. It is neutrality of judgments that will help us return to our realization of who we really are.

There are situations and circumstances that may seem tragic that end in wonderful spiritual alignments and growth. This doesn't mean you should pay someone to torture you just so you can have spiritual growth.

It seems that there are many that choose the path of non-resistance to evil simply because they are trying to fool the world into believing they are practicing a Divine Principle, when in fact they are manipulating their audience to pay them for nothing.

Staying in the Divine Matrix of Virtual Reality

Many people on earth think they are living in the Divine Matrix of Virtual Reality when in fact they are living in the Matrix of Illusions. Each person needs to examine their thoughts each day to make sure their thoughts are reflecting the Divine Reality rather than the illusions that the world would like to implant in our minds.

The Matrix of Illusions can easily be mistaken for the Matrix of Reality because to those only trained in material concepts, these mortal dreams are the only reality available to their consciousness. Those who do not have a spiritually directed background probably can't see the difference between spiritual reality and material reality. Unfortunately, many of those living the divine life are also confused between the divinity of God and the illusions created by our government and society that make us believe our nation represents the divine qualities of God. People are often confused between what is considered good by society and government and what is, by nature, good because it comes from God. Churches have been able to be used by governments for centuries to support very non-divine activities because of this confusion. This confusion is a doorway for abuse that is eagerly and freely used by governments and those in positions of power.

How to Survive on Earth

I believe it is the art of seeing beyond cultural beliefs into the unity of oneness that is required before the mastery of oneness and ascension. While I believe it is valid and extremely helpful to continue looking at this gift of compassion in the light of physics, I believe it is also imperative that we each begin the journey of a cultural anthropologist and socio-linguist in order to better understand the reasons and the necessity for our lives and our language to become totally jumbled into the language of Babel where we have become pieces of a puzzle that must be reorganized into the divine plan of who we actually are in order to return to our oneness with our divine plan of creation.

Programmed Reality

The program that we have created here on earth has separated us from the original Garden of Eden, where every spiritual reality was already prepared for us. We have chosen to have control of our own world. We have become brainwashed to believe that this is the actual world that we were created in and live in, when in fact it is only a program of our minds that has been connected through electronic vibrations to lower us into the dream of material sense. When the vibrations are raised back to the speed of light, (which is what our real vibrations are) we return to our state of oneness

with our true creation. We have already examined many ways
of returning from the Matrix of Illusions to the Matrix of
Reality. This can be done by returning to Before the World
began to the Promise of the Perfect Kingdom. It can be done
by staying in the Now Zone. It can be done by pulling out all
of the roots from the Garden of Eden in which we ate of the
tree of good and evil, and planting them back in the Divine
Creation. The Quantum Journey writings and courses have
examined in detail the ways we can return to our Divine Right
of the Perfect Kingdom.

There is an even more important tool that will help wash our
past illusions away. The tool that keeps us in the Divine
Reality is the announcement of, the practice of, the
realization of, and the bringing forth of LOVE. Divine Love
has always been meeting our needs and has never stopped
meeting our needs. We stop the Divine Love from doing its
thing when we block Divine Reality through Mortal Illusions.

I can think of a million times when I have blocked even my
own mother's love by believing that I would be better off
doing something other than what she was directing me to do
because she loved me so much. As children, we think it is
better if we get to eat all of the candy that our mother tells us
not to eat. We think it is better to go play on the street that
our mother directs us through her love not to play on. Later
in life, we think we are better off riding in fast cars with
popular wild teenagers than staying home where it is safe, as
our mothers love wishes we would do.

Making Divine Love's Movie

We do the same thing constantly to our Spiritual Mother who
is the Eternal Life Force preparing, generating and enfolding
us in the White Light that we are created of. We choose to
become mortal creatures instead of the White Light that we
actually are. We deny the Divine Love that is waiting patiently
to serve us and guide us every time we choose to serve the

world's beliefs, the government's beliefs, the educator's beliefs rather than the Divine Reality that propels our being into existence. Divine Love tells us not to eat of the tree of knowledge of good and evil, so what do we spend our lives doing? Has one day gone by in your life when you did not eat of the tree of knowledge of good and evil? Have you taken up the belief that there is a reality other than the Divine Life Force?

We have all done this, and continue to do so every day. When we stop doing this, we will return to the Divine Reality. We also block this Love from radiating from our being by spending most our thoughts on material lies that cause us to react rather than radiate. We must practice replacing reactions with radiations. Each time someone does an unloving deed, we must react with Love rather than react with fear, hatred, violence or revenge. We must radiate Divine Love at such a high vibration that no other reality has the time to break through this radiation.

We can become a constant radiation of Love by constantly staying in the Now Zone where there is no other thought or reaction except the constant listening for the guidance and direction of the Life Force. As we allow ourselves to become a vehicle for the Life Force to radiate through, we must constantly radiate this same Life Force into action through our own Divine Love. As we become beacons of White Light, we become the Divine Love that appears as supply, as friendship, as the givers of Eternal Life.

We can begin placing the radiation into action by doing little deeds of love each hour of the day. We can radiate more and more as we let go of the illusions that are blocking our love from radiating. We can radiate at the speed of light when we allow the Life Force to have total possession of our beings, and to ride on the energy, power and forgiveness of the Life Force of Universal Energy. We can become the White Light Energy that brings all material illusions back into the focus of their Divine Reality. This is how all spiritual healing is done.

We must first become White Light, demonstrate White Light and see everyone we meet as White Light to demonstrate the Spiritual Healing that we are all capable of. As we keep our minds stayed on the Oneness of the one white light cell that is the Divine Creation of all being, we become the white light radiating from the Life Force, and we can see everyone on earth as this white light that we all are.

This constant radiation of Divine Being in the form of Love is the most powerful force in all of the universes. We each contain the power of Divine Love. We each contain the Divine Matrix of Reality that we must radiate outward. We must practice radiating Love first in a field that can be felt by ourselves and others. Next, we must radiate Love to other nations that need Love in various forms. Finally, we must radiate Love into Infinity, and it will return as Infinite Love to ourselves and to all who are receptive to our healing influence. This is our Divine right and duty as children of Divine Love.

Love is Kind

Sometimes the translation of Love appears as charity, sometimes as compassion, and sometimes as kindness or forgiveness. Love is always in the form of an action. Love can be a silent, contemplative action, but it is always an action. We must express Love. We must radiate Love. The more we radiate Love, the more the Life Force will contact us personally because we have raised our vibrations closer to the reality of our White Light. Love can only reflect Love. We must radiate first and then we become available. The Angel of Love can only be heard by those who have their minds stayed on Love.

Removing the Challenge

Each time we are confronted with a messenger or a challenger on this earth, it is because something in our program is indirectly connected to this charge that will help propel us back to our source of oneness. It is not the Source that brings us guidance through pain. However, this pain is brought on by our own individual programming that wants to return to our original speed of light vibration. The more we see each challenge on earth as a non-challenge to our reality, the more the programmed world will seem an unreality until we finally return to our state of reality.

The Non Power

In the movie The Matrix there were Agents, programs that looked like people, that moved through the Matrix in order to keep the people under control. The Matrix was a program of a material artificial world that tricked people into believing that it was reality in order to control their every thought and action, and they lived out their lives in this artificial dream. Neo, the hero of the movie, woke up from the artificial dream and then worked to free everyone. We must prove, as Neo proved, that the program of materiality around us actually has no power over us. When Neo was able to see the nothingness of the Agents, the non-power of their being began to be his reality. Neo represented the same sense of Christ that Jesus Christ presented to us in His movie on earth. Christ showed us the non-power of the world just as Neo showed us the non-power of the world. Few have caught on to Christ's teachings over the past two thousand years, and few will catch on to Neo's symbolism, probably not even the writers of the movie, who are only concerned with creating animated action heroes.

If we are actually the speed of light, the ability to fight faster than the fastest material fighter becomes a simple non-action because we are already the speed of light, which can't in reality be touched by the material Agent. As Neo learned from the child in the Oracle's house, the spoon doesn't bend - it is only our mind that bends around the spoon. The action fighting Agent doesn't move or bend either - it is only Neo's mind that was bending around the Agent. Because in reality, we are the reflection of the Divine Creator - not something separate - and if not separate - than nothing exists except our divine reflection of infinite being. Where is the Agent that can destroy infinite being? That Agent only exists as a programmed belief in our minds. It is a belief that has been programmed by the material sense - or the Matrix. It looses power and looses control of our minds when we choose to pull the plugs out of our brains and reconnect our minds with our oneness - our speed of light existence.

Course 16

Dear Fellow Aliens

I am writing this letter to my fellow beings on my planet of origination. I left my planet and began my journey about 50 years ago. I am wondering if anyone has missed me back home. I am sending you this story because I think it is important for you to know a few things about the experience you will have when you get here, as well as the transformation you will go through as you change from white light into a lower vibration of mortality. Since we all seem to have our minds deleted when we return home, I'm sure most of you do not remember your journey to earth. I've had so much of my Divine Matrix erased by this planet, that I can't even remember the name of our planet of white light–I will call you the Matrix of Reality. I thought I would share some of my experiences with you so you will know what to expect when it is your turn to come here, and show you how to make sure you can find your way back home when you are finished with your journey.

We must all realize that these earth people have been living a life among aliens, just as I have learned that I have been. We don't know for sure if they are aliens from another planet, or if they are just aliens to the existence of humanity and acting as human beings, or if they are aliens to their true existence as the white light which prepared a blueprint to be performed on earth. The sad reality is we have all become aliens to each other and even to our true selves. We have allowed the matrix of the world to rewrite the blueprints that were originally established in our minds. When the spiritual blueprint is written into material form, the essence of our oneness which allowed us to live in harmony as one interwoven being which understands and loves empathetically its entire being of Man, is deleted. When our true essence is deleted, we become as a blank computer disk waiting to have new trivia placed upon it, in whatever form it comes. When the true form no longer knows that it is in reality a perfectly formulated mapping using pure white light to constantly regenerate every cell in its bodily form through eternity, it begins to degenerate into the nothingness that the matrix of illusions defines it to be.

Shape Shifters

I was born into a family of aliens. They were aliens to me and I was an alien to them. I knew from the beginning that my vibrations were being lowered from the spiritual vibration of the speed of light down into a form that took on a human shape. Inside the matrix that I was assigned to on earth, I felt a vibration so slow and dark that I was born crying and continued to cry daily for the first part of my life. I had already gone through the terrible experience of shape shifting from the pure white light that enjoyed the infinity of being into a very tiny form enveloped by the belief of flesh. Inside this flesh I knew my true self still existed in the form of white light. This was when I was still being blessed by the guidance of my pineal gland, my third eye, which held me in direct contact with my true creator. My shape was being shifted and modified second by second by the shape shifters that brought me into their matrix and planted the belief of their genetic genes into me. Of course, I never did believe they could change my essence of reality, which had already been formed in the world of white light, only to have my vibrations temporarily lowered so that I could be of service on earth.

When I first opened my eyes, after going through this terrifying process of shape shifting into a mortal form, there were these big people waiting for me and one of them picked me up by the feet and slapped me on my behind. I thought to myself, "I was obviously sent to hell by accident. What did I do wrong? I thought my creator loved me and I was only moments ago being expressed as the white light of Divine Mind. Now my form has been lowered into this ugly thing with skin and fat. I can understand why these people would be so angry. I must be deformed or something."

Well, it never got any better. Those people who were waiting to welcome me into their hell continued to be disgusted with my form. They complained about me every day of my life. They even started referring to me as your daughter, no your daughter, no your daughter, no your daughter. And then as that "crying, spoiled baby." The only time they stopped complaining about me was when they went to sleep. As soon as they woke up, it started all over again. They complained that they had to feed me. They complained they had to change my diapers. They complained they had to stop me from crying. Finally they just said, just let her cry, maybe she'll dry up eventually.

Then there was this other alien that came into my life. He was a little shorter than the other two people who constantly complained about me. He didn't seem to like me very much, either. He was always angry that the other big people were always playing with me instead of him. He was always sulking.

After I had been living on earth long enough that the big people felt they had control of me they started sharing me with other people. They would pass me around in my blanket and all of these other people would smile, make faces, squeeze my cheek and make funny sounds. These people seemed to like me a lot more than the ones that were always complaining about me. I always looked forward to the big people taking me out of their house and leaving me with people who liked me. Every time we returned to their house, the vibrations in the house seemed much lower than they did outside. It felt like there was none of the white light vibrations that I had lived in before. They acted like they were constantly upset that I had intruded in on their life. When the shorter one played with me he always hurt me and I'd start crying, and then the big ones would make him cry. Pretty soon he didn't play with me any more, and he wouldn't talk to me for years.

This new adventure of transforming to a mortal being had been extremely painful so far. I can't imagine why I would have written such a terrible movie for my being of white light to be placed into. It was very different on this planet than the way things had been back home. All of the creations were in the form of white light, all of these individual forms interacted with each other harmoniously. Everything that one had belonged to the other. There were never any problems and there was always love. This new planet seemed like it had all of the light and love sucked out of it, and everyone wanted to take on these different forms instead of everyone looking the same. There weren't many of the qualities that I used to enjoy back home like truth, joy, intelligence, principle, understanding, love and harmony. On this planet the forms preferred to use untruth, a lack of joy, very little intelligence, absolutely no principle behind anything said or done, they certainly didn't try to understand me nor themselves. Their love was translated into food and their highest understanding of harmony was when they stopped yelling and began pouting. Such an unhappy planet I had been assigned to.

My Blueprint on Earth

I had begun my assignment on earth to go through the daily interactions with aliens that would help guide me in achieving the victory of leaving my blueprint on earth that would help others remember and return to the wonderful home planet of white light. Whatever I was experiencing with these aliens was part of the blueprint that I had written on the other side before I had shifted from white light vibrations into fleshly form. This was all part of the plan that would result in the ultimate victory of freedom from the matrix of illusions.

The only reason that life on earth would appear to be, or turn out to be less than fruitful, or even painful is because these big people are trying to program me to look at life through their blueprints instead of the ones that I had personally designed for myself before leaving the other side.

Many think that they have begun their life on earth and in several decades this life will end. Some think they will vanish into thin air and others think they will be eternally punished at the end of their time. These variables of not knowing what is at the end, is a reason for constant fear for many. I've certainly had my moments and even days of fear and wondering why am I here? Why do I have to be here? Why do I have to go through the pain of life just to reach some fearful unknown of death.

Yes, even aliens have these thoughts. And I have always known that death is unreal and that most of life is an illusion. I've known that fact since I was two years old when I started Sunday School. I had learned at a very young age that life is eternal and that I live every second of my life in God's omnipresent love, protection, guidance and principle. This was not new knowledge for me, but it seems that way when we don't remember.

Fear

So, where do these attacks of fear and confusion come from?
Sometimes they come from having no tangible evidence of
the very belief that my life is based on. And where does that
come from? It comes from closing my eyes to all of the
evidence of that belief.

Why would I want to close my eyes to that wonderful belief
that I've had continuous proof of? The word is fear. Fear is
like a negation of what is actually here. Fear comes from
people telling us things that contradict our truth. Fear comes
from illusions of pain and death that destroy the reality we
believe. Fear starts when we shift from the speed of light
vibration down to a very slow vibration that can only be seen
by my mortality. This slow vibration makes us feel trapped
because we were used to flying at the speed of light before the
transformation.

How do we turn the fear around, destroy the fear and return
to our wonderful belief we learned in Sunday School? It
certainly requires faith, believing, strength and, most of all,
remembering all of the positive proof that we've already been
given. An even easier way is to remember, that in reality, we
still are white light, we still are traveling at the speed of light,
and it is only the eyes of the mortal that is transforming the
reality into the matrix of illusions.

Matrix of Reality

If we simply kept a journal every day that records the proof of
the guidance, protection, love that we experience, we could
look at that journal when Mr. Fear comes around. I began
keeping a journal of these proofs in my head when I was four
or five years old and every few years I sit and write down all of
those stories that show that proof. I think it is the very fact
that I continuously look for proof, seek for evidence and
know that I could have such a perfect understanding of my

life, why I'm here, what I'm supposed to do every day, as well as know all of eternity, before I placed myself back into the world in order to remember every past life I've lived and the reasons I keep returning to earth, and to even know about others lives if I need to.

You probably don't meet many people that believe that they are actually blessed with that much knowledge. You probably don't meet that many people that will admit they are aliens, either. We all possess the knowledge of reality. We all know how to escape the matrix of illusions. We all know how to return to the speed of light. However, we spend so much time entertaining the matrix of illusions that we forget that we could be spending our time in the Matrix of Reality. Some would even say that much knowledge is very unhealthy and it is certainly unhealthy to the world we think we live in because that knowledge would destroy most of the illusions that give doctors, lawyers and funeral owners their jobs.

There is certainly plenty of evidence of prophets and visionaries and mystics recorded in the Bible, the Koran and other records of the spiritual man. There is also plenty of evidence of masters, visionaries and psychics showing us the path to our personal blueprints. Some of us have been so blessed that we've been guided by aliens, angels, psychics and spirit guides without ever asking to be or even believing in such a thing.

The Journey

The church through which my spiritual understanding came and grew would certainly never permit me to talk to a psychic. My church would condemn such an action, as most churches would. My church and all churches condemn communication with aliens, witches, angels, spirit guides, or any other being that would take away their power that enables them to be the only one that we have the right to believe. The purpose of any church is to contain all truth, guidance and direction in it and it alone. The purpose of every church is to prepare a place for the sheep to graze. We are to remain sheep and remain under the guidance of that church. That is certainly what I believed for about forty years. I believed that only my church and the teachers in my church held the true story of reality and healing.

My uncle, who had always seemed like an angel to me, invited me into his house in L.A. I didn't even know why there was concern about me in my family since I had never had a kind or compassionate word said to me by them in times of need in the past. When anyone in my family has a problem and admits it, they are automatically considered insane, so I assume my uncle took me to a psychic because he either thought I had a mental problem or some emotional problem, or it could had even been to get secret information about what why I wanted to know how much money was in the stock my family bought for me. Members of my family were always trying to prove some other member was crazy or a liar. It always revolved around money. A person begins to wonder if he is telling the truth or not when surrounded by people who are always twisting stories around to make another look like a liar. I spent years watching myself so closely, and making sure that I was the most honest person on earth because these people made me so paranoid. Nonetheless, I never questioned my family's actions or demands, I just went along with whatever came my way. I was under their manipulative mind control, and had been for many years - probably starting the time I began using my pituitary gland instead of my pineal gland, which had previously connected my thoughts and vibrations directly to my creator.

This psychic told me that there was no future relationship with the boy I was dating and she told me that I would never go to Russia or use the Russian language that I had been studying as a Russian major in college. She told me that I was interested in the Russian language and had a pull to return to Asia because of unfinished business in a past life. She told me I would definitely be returning to Asia, but not Russia. She said I had several past lives relating to history involving several countries in Asia, mostly east Asia.

She said she could clearly see me returning to the same places I had lived before and meeting those same people who had left me with unresolved issues in my life. She also told me that the person I would marry lived near my home town, attended a school near my home and we would meet at that school. She said she was pretty sure we had already met before at that school or near that school, but I may not have even realized who he was.

When I left the psychic's home, I seriously considered the possibility of my present relationship being the wrong one because that's what I wanted to hear. I didn't really take her seriously, however. I had been taught in church that there is no reason to believe there are past lives because there is only one life. And I was totally sure she was wrong about meeting my husband at some school near my home because I had no intentions of returning home and going to a community college because I was attending UC Davis and planned on returning to Illinois to finish college.

I did finish college in Illinois; and, I did return to California to try to get a job that related to my major in music. I changed my major from Russian to music because the counselor at UC Davis told me that I would have to get a double major in economics if I ever wanted to use the Russian language. Well, I hate economics, politics and all subjects relating to accounting or numbers. So, the Russian language clearly had no place in my life.

After attempting several jobs including piano sales, piano bar player, tutor and waitress, a great opportunity came up to sell education for a technical school back in my home town. I moved home, began my new job and two weeks later, the job was eliminated because the school didn't think there was enough business in that area. So, I started giving piano lessons to make money and started pursuing a masters degree in music at the local college. After taking a few jazz classes, I decided to sign up at a community college to play with a jazz band.

So, I did end up going to the college near my home - just as the psychic said I would. When I was sitting at the piano and looked around the room, while the conductor was introducing me as the new pianist for the band, I looked at the trombone player and the first thought that came to my mind was "I'm going to marry him." No, it wasn't love at first sight. I just knew I was going to marry him.

Probably the same way the psychic knew that I was going to marry this person that I would meet in a college near my parent's home, and whom I had nearly met in another college nearby a few years earlier. The first day of the jazz band class, the trombone player asked me if I'd like to go to a Thad Jones jazz concert with him that weekend. Joe and I went to the Thad Jones concert in San Francisco that weekend and the next week I told him we were getting married and four months later we were married.

I still didn't believe in psychics, but I sure thought it was interesting that she had told me that I'd meet my husband in the school nearby my home and that I had already been in the same school with him before. The psychic was right on both points - I had attended Chico State as a music major my sophomore year. Joe's brother was a trumpet major at that time and I was a piano accompanist for a friend of his who tried very hard to set me up on a date with him. The musician I accompanied repeatedly told me that he thought I should be with the brother of his friend. That was the exact connection the psychic had described. I still didn't take the coincidence very seriously because I certainly didn't believe in past lives or reincarnation. And I still held to the belief planted in my mind by my church that psychics were phonies.

My husband and I lived in his grandmother's trailer, I taught piano lessons and he was a land surveyor. We continued to be active in music by participating in bands and musical comedies. We even started our own performing art center and a newspaper. Our income couldn't sustain us, so we joined the Air Force.

We ended up being stationed in South Korea as computer operators. The military life didn't support our religious beliefs very well, so we were out of there in less than six months. But, we had been placed in Korea, the place I was obviously destined to return to according to the psychic.

Little did I know, my journey back to my previous lives had begun, and I was about to repeat all of the same human interactions that had required me to draw a new blueprint of my life that would allow me to correct and complete the unfinished business from previous lives. Of course, I didn't believe any of this nonsense at the time. I was getting hundreds of glimpses of my past dreams of dragons, encounters with the year of the dragon, encounters with attempts of murder on my life, along with a deep sense of mystery, drama, larger than life experience where the clues that this was not just a normal life, but some journey back into the past, as if I were trapped in a time machine.

I had totally forgotten that I was an alien by this time. I had forgotten that I had recently been transformed from white light into this fleshly substance of the world's matrix. And I had most definitely forgotten the last hundred times that I had gone through this same transformation of life forms and life stories.

What was suddenly making me remember many of my past life stories? I think the key word is familiarity. I had a familiarity - a deep understanding of Korea, its history, its people and a feeling that this was the correct way to live and I had this familiar feeling that I had returned home.

I started feeling more and more that the things the psychic said could be true. Apparently, while I was on the Other Side,

I chose two themes to guide my journey. In my blueprint of this life I chose the themes of rejection and spirituality. I also seem to have a theme of intellectuality that pushes me to want to thoroughly research the cause of these other two themes in my life.

Blueprint Themes for Success

I had always resented my parents for bringing me into this world because I thought I was brought here totally against my will, and forced to live in to a world full of rejection everywhere I turned. I thought my search for my return to spiritual oneness was set off by the pain my family caused me through their rejection. Even though I knew I was an alien, and they had no idea that they didn't really create me, I thought they should be a lot nicer to a foreign visitor.

Of course, they never saw it this way. For them, I was more of a plaything, a scapegoat, someone to blame everything on, someone to create lies about. I just set myself up as this easy target because I was trained to believe that everything was as perfect as the kingdom of heaven that I had just come from. My mother would claim she loved me, even though she never seemed to care when I cried all night long because I was so confused, frightened and very unhappy. I would believe her because I knew my true mother to be God, and God certainly did love me.

It wasn't until I had spent almost 50 years of my life blaming my pain on my family that I learned that it was I who had written my own blueprint establishing myself into whatever early childhood rejection, torture all through school, rejection in every work situation and human relationship that I encountered. I wrote this blueprint to ensure the ultimate success of my other theme - spirituality. It has always been the continuous rejection in my life that has resulted in the successful progress I've made in spiritual growth. This rejection kept me from having a narrow mindedness in my spiritual journey. I was even rejected by my church, which caused me to search farther and wider, be more cautious and more compassionate and empathetic to others' spiritual beliefs. The rejection of my pursuits in healing music caused me to be broader in my means and methods of conveying and sharing my healing messages in a format that might appeal to a greater population of spiritual seekers and others who have been rejected or persecuted without ever being told that they wrote these themes into their own blueprints before they came here from the other side.

What was most helpful to me was the gift that my uncle gave me when he took me to that psychic in L.A. If I hadn't been told ahead of time by this psychic that my uncle took me to see, I wouldn't had known the significance of what happened to me when I lived in Korea and in Japan. I knew that the events that happened during my journey to these countries was extremely significant to my spiritual growth, but I would had never realized that the feelings of deja vu that I had been rejected and probably killed by these same people that I again chose to be rejected by in previous life times. It even seemed as though my persecutors were trying their best to keep me from leading myself to the slaughter once again, but apparently I had written rejection and persecution into my blueprints in previous life times as well.

Maybe my theme on the other side was to be a perfectionist at establishing my mirror image of oneness with God, so I keep coming back to earth because I want to keep refining my spiritual strength to the point of total oneness. My religion taught me that it is actually easier to learn healing oneness and to gain all spiritual growth while on this earth. Apparently, the other side offers no real challenges because all is perfection and oneness. I can imagine no other reason for sending myself back to these lives of rejection and persecution at least three times that I can clearly remember. My most vivid memories are of my lifetimes in Korea and in Japan. I remember living in Korea before at a time in history when Korean men took a "little wife" to bear their children and then destroyed them. It was also a time in history when female babies were often thrown into the ocean because only male children were desired. I remember living in Japan when geisha girls were the talented, well-educated females that Japanese men had their intellectual discussions with and often fell in love with, but they were forced to live a life of denial and shame because the real wives were all that existed "in reality."

Desire to Help

My desire to help my fellow aliens understand is a result of several years of searching and researching life on earth in various cultural groups. Just as leaving my home planet and coming to earth was a great culture shock, so was living in different cultures and going through the same mind shifts over and over again. Those of you who have forgotten that you have ever lived anywhere else will have the hardest time lifting your minds from the narrow existence that you have let the matrix trap you into. The matrix of illusions will make you forget everything in your past and resent anything that is unlike the self your little tiny culture that you live within has created for you. The few who do no get trapped become self actualized and can see the equal value of all ways of life, but most of the lost aliens will remain in a very small mind with very narrow viewpoints programmed into them. If these programs are not broken, there will be little chance of ever leaving the earth and returning home to our white light.

Write in Your Journal

Please begin writing in your journal. Begin your story of your life as you remember, beginning with your memories of coming into this world. Start remembering all of the strange coincidences and deja vu feelings that might spark your memory of your past lives, as well the reason you were sent back to earth this time. This book is intended to help you begin to see that the experiences that are being planted in your head in this world are not necessary reality, but movies that are being projected from others' minds as well as the minds of your past lives. Start separating the illusions from the realities each day, until you finally remember who you really are. Work to free yourselves from the Matrix of Illusions so you can know and live from who you truly are.

Finale

 Sometimes people feel that if they learn more about spirituality and make it a part of their lives, their lives will become easier and run more smoothly in their everyday lives. What has to be realized is that learning about spirituality and making it a part of one's life requires coming out of the Matrix of Illusions of the world around the person. This sometimes puts a person at odds with the norm and with the society as a whole. Becoming spiritual does not make one more popular. Jesus Christ was the most obvious example of this. Christ Jesus was finally hung on a cross by people hypnotized by the existing Matrixes of Illusions of that time.

 The world has the tendency to want to remain asleep because if they wake up, the world as they know it will disappear. By coming out of the world - out of the Matrices of Illusions that are all around us - we are often met face-to-face with those deep down into the illusions who fight to keep their dream alive. However, those who are on a spiritual path can be protected from harms way through the all power of Divine Reality that we work to live within at all times.

 Divine Reality is real and we can and do live and have our being there. We must learn how to recognize the Matrixes of

Illusions and understand how they work so we are not inadvertently lulled to sleep by them unknowingly. The Matrix of Illusions is often very subtle and appears as something good and natural even though it is not. Sometimes the Illusions seem harmless, and they are, as long as we know that they are illusions and do not put too much weight on following them. The trick is to stay in Divine Reality at all times and live, move and always have our being there as we move through life on a daily basis.

Do we need to join a church or a group to live out from Divine Reality? No. Divine Reality is not contained in a church or organization. Human organizations often work as a Matrix of Illusions that sets up many rules about spirituality that have little to do with Divine Reality and have more to do with belonging to their exclusive club. Divine Reality is known by the individual - not by a group or organization; it is a Divine relationship between the individual and the Infinite that is only known within. The Divine Relationship is so powerful, it boggles the mind that is asleep in the Matrix of Illusions and cannot be comprehended or fathomed. Only people who have experienced the Matrix of Reality, even if just a little, can understand the infinite power and possibilities that are known there.

The spiritual path is not always easier, but it is always real. Once a person starts to know Reality, going back down to sleep into a waking dream seems ridiculous and a waste of time and effort. Substance and value are only known through Divine Reality - it cannot be known or experienced anywhere else or in any other way. An illusion will always feel superficial and unsatisfying - it will always feel like there is something missing because it is only an illusion, which pops like a bubble when Reality is seen, known, and lived from. The Matrix of Reality can only be known as one begins the journey out from under the thumb and hypnotism of the Matrix of Illusions and into the freedom of Divine Reality.

The best of everything for you on your journey into Reality!!